Linda L.

Strangers into Friends

Hospitality as Mission

Abingdon Press / Nashville

Strangers into Friends: Hospitality as Mission

by Linda L. Pickens-Jones

Copyright © 1999 by Abingdon Press

ISBN 0-687-03240-7

This book is printed on acid-free paper.

99 00 01 02 03 04 05 06 07 08—10 9 8 7 6 5 4 3 2 1

MANUFACTURED IN THE UNITED STATES OF AMERICA

Contents

The Rev. Dr. Linda L. Pickens-Jones has had experiences in all areas of pastoral ministry, including working in cross-cultural communities and providing retreat leadership. She has served as a missionary through the General Board of Global Ministries for The United Methodist Church in Sierra Leone, West Africa, where she was also director of youth ministry for the national church. She has served as pastor at Venice United Methodist Church in Los Angeles and San Bruno United Methodist Church, where she developed a cooperative ministry plan with the Tongan congregation. Between 1987 and 1991, she worked on program development and implementation for fifty churches in the urban Los Angeles district of The United Methodist Church. Currently she pastors Community United Methodist Church of Millbrae.

Dr. Pickens-Jones obtained her doctor of ministry and her master of divinity degrees at the School of Theology at Claremont. She served in the California-Pacific Annual Conference from 1977 to 1998 and is currently a member of California-Nevada Annual Conference. She has published seven articles on mission and has been a staff writer for *FaithLink*. She has served as a keynote and conference speaker at several church-related gatherings and retreats. In 1998 she was appointed trainer of the Diversity Initiative for the California-Nevada Annual Conference Counsel for the Church.

A Word of Welcome

Welcome to *Strangers into Friends: Hospitality as Mission.*
This five-session study will introduce you to the faithful practice of hospitality and to several ordinary persons or occasions in the Bible which, with God's help, successfully brought about extraordinary things. Our first hope is that your experience in the study group will be a gift, an act of hospitality to you. You probably have plenty to do; you are giving—perhaps sacrificing—your time to participate. We hope there is a blessing in it for all of you.

Being and Doing

You may be attending Vacation Bible School with your child. He or she will be studying the same "can-do" characters as you and in the same order. The children will learn that God gives the wisdom and power, even to children and youth, to accomplish wonderful acts of ministry. It is important for our young people to learn that they "can do," too.

As adults, we know you can "do." In fact, you have probably already been called to do, and do some more, and then to do even more. We hope your experience with this study will encourage you to *be*—be in relationship with God, be aware of how God works through ordinary people, be mindful of the needs for compassion and hospitality in the world. If, as a result, you feel led by God to *do*, God will provide the means and the ways. Hospitality is first of all a way of being and then a means to doing.

The Long and Short of It

You may instead be participating in this study in a church school group or midweek study. Whether in the short or long format, this study is adaptable to your needs.

Each session has a core passage studied by the other age levels in "Club Can-Do." The core lesson material offers teaching activities and suggestions in the margins. The core activities are noted in the narrow margin with the icon ❖, indicating the teaching helps basic to the section in the main text to which they refer. You can choose from among them to plan a 40–50 minute session, although using all of them will take much longer.

To develop an extended session, add more of these activities and/or use the alternative activities under that heading. Teaching helps noted in **bold italics** take longer to do and/or will take some added preparation time during or before the session to tap more creatively into the menu of teaching options.

All persons learn in a variety of ways. When you select the questions and activities for discussion and reflection, we suggest you keep in mind a number of approaches. Use a mixture of questions that ask for fact, interpretation, analysis, reflection, and application. Add activities that use the senses and allow for creative expression, for example, through drama, writing, or storytelling.

Let This Be a Gift

Encourage participants to use their heads and their hearts in studying and applying the Scriptures so that they delve into more than just an examination of the text. Help group members experience the "so what" of this study so that they are better able to see God at work in the world and God at work in themselves and others. There are numerous stories of personal and intercultural experiences that add richness and flavor to the topic. Establish an atmosphere that urges all participants to share their own stories.

This study, especially in conjunction with "Club Can-Do," will encourage persons of all ages to engage in hospitality that flows into missional action as a natural and eager response to God's particular call to them. True hospitality is a gift, not a burden. We hope you experience this time as a blessing.

Biblical Hospitality

$\mathcal{S}$trangers become friends. Travelers become guests. Hunger and thirst are satisfied. Souls and bodies find nourishment and honor. Such is the course of hospitality.

Hospitality in the Bible

Travelers through the desert in Old Testament days relied on an elaborate code of hospitality based on testing and trust, receiving and reciprocity. In dry, hot climates with villages at some distance from each other, finding a place for food, water, and shelter was a matter of life and death. Natives of a herding society were forced to rely on the generosity of their "neighbors," whether of their own community or ethnic origin or foreigners.

While notions of hospitality shifted some over the course of Old and New Testament times, and from a herding to agricultural to urban culture, being a good host continued to engender trust with a traveler whose own people might one day be asked for hospitality by the host. On the other hand, being a poor host or a poor guest seriously jeopardized the possibility of finding a hospitable welcome elsewhere.

From Stranger to Friend

Travel was dangerous, and even more so in the days of ancient Israel. Some centuries later, during the relative protection ushered in by the Roman Empire in early church days, travel was a less risky business. Nevertheless, persons did not necessarily mix well with someone from another tribe, city, or culture and thus posed a potential danger. Strangers were received, sometimes with suspicion, and tested to see how they would accommodate to the norms of their host community.

Testing the Stranger

Community leaders could, and sometimes did, ask strangers to move on. For example, Jesus was unwelcome among the Gerasenes. They were afraid of what he had done to their herd of pigs, possibly fearing a similar fate would befall them (Mark 5:14-20). They pleaded with him to leave, and he did.

When a stranger was tested and found welcome, he became a guest. The ritual footwashing was a sign of acceptance and movement to this next stage as guest (Genesis 18:1-4).

From Stranger to Guest

Strangers had no social or legal standing in a new community. While letters of recommendation may have assisted in the transition from stranger to guest, these persons were still vulnerable. They needed the patronage and protection of an established resident, such as Lot offered the angelic visitors in Genesis 19:1-11. When his guests were threatened, Lot as a host was also threatened.

To modern eyes, the protection Lot offered seems extreme, yet it was for its time an excellent example of the extent to which the good host would go to care for guests. They were more important than the host or his property (Lot's daughters) in that culture. The good host would willingly give generously to his guest as Abraham had done with his angelic visitors (Genesis 18:1-8).

Generosity on the part of either guest or host did not always prevent a breach of etiquette. Guests could inappropriately assume the role of host, rival another guest, give orders to the host's servants, or otherwise insult the host. By failing to offer

8

any of the expected signs of hospitality—food, drink, footwashing, shelter, or respect—the host could just as easily offend the guest and compromise the possibility of receiving hospitality later when the host was in the role of guest. For example, Simon the Pharisee woefully neglected his invited guest Jesus. Although a man of some community standing, Simon's hospitality toward Jesus was far less gracious and generous than that offered by the uninvited woman who cleaned Jesus' feet with her hair (Luke 7:36-46).

From Guest to Friend

A guest left the host's temporary sanctuary either as a friend or an enemy. If he had been treated well, the guest would certainly report on the host favorably, at least to the sending person or community. A friend was gained, and a relationship was established.

If he had been rejected or treated with dishonor, the aggrieved guest would certainly report that as well. The sending community might be expected to treat the host or his neighbor as an enemy. Retaliation, rather than hospitable reciprocity, could be the result of a serious breach by the host. "When his own received him not," Jesus chose not to strike back. When rejected by Nabal (1 Samuel 25), David was swayed from avenging the insult only by the quick-witted and generous response of Abigail, Nabal's wife.

The Hospitality of Home

In Jesus' day and in the first century, hospitality took on a different nuance; travel was easier and safer, thanks to an extensive system of inns. These accommodations were often minimal, so the warmth and generosity of the home maintained a high importance. Jesus was a frequent guest, and these homes provided the setting for much of his teaching.

For example, Paul's letters often mention the practice of expecting and finding shelter in the home of a new convert, such as Lydia (Acts 16:11-15, 40), or a believer. Indeed, the practice of hospitality was—and still is—regarded as a mark of faith and Christian love (Romans 12:9-13).

Truths for Those Not from the Desert

Is this intricate social dance from "stranger to guest to friend or enemy" relevant for an urbane, modern society where doors are locked and strangers, especially ones not "like me," are often held in suspicion? Are not persons still in need of food and drink, of shelter and protection, of respect from neighbors, who might initially be strangers? This biblical concept and practice of hospitality has a lot of life left in it because it shows us several timeless truths for the community of faith.

✤ At some time or other, hospitality comes knocking at your door (like the angels who came to Abraham and Lot and who turned out, in fact, to be their protectors). You no doubt have received a word fitly spoken, a gift unexpected, a warning well-timed, a gesture of comfort badly needed, from a neighbor—or even from a stranger—who saw your need.

✤ Hospitality is expected of us as long as there are strangers, travelers, and those who are poor monetarily or in spirit. Although we can choose to offer it or not, our Scriptures require it (Romans 12:13).

✤ Hospitality is an action. Guests and hosts alike will always make judgments on how well they have been treated. We might even be immortalized as good hosts (like Jesus, who washed his disciples' feet in John 13:1-20) or as poor hosts (like Simon in Luke 7:36-50).

✤ Hospitality is mutual. In a world made smaller and smaller each day with every CNN newscast, the impact of our concern for others (or lack of it) cannot be overlooked. When we do embrace the opportunity to be generous with our time, money, talent, and especially with ourselves, we often find in that a great personal blessing.

I Know All That, But I'm Really Busy

You yourself need a blessing. You are probably fragmented with responsibilities at home, at work, and at church. Now you are beginning a new study, which will at least require your presence with the rest of the study group. You may hunger for more time with your family and also thirst for enrichment and spiritual nurture from your faith.

Consider yourself a guest at a gathering at which God is your host. Expect refreshment from engaging in a study of these biblical stories so that you can become better acquainted with your Host. Look for signs of God's presence in the other participants and draw from their personal stories and experiences of God's love. Expect to transform from stranger to friend with the others who study and reflect with you. Offer your own insight to complement theirs.

Think of this time together as a gift. If God calls you to offer yourself as host in mission and caring to a stranger, you will know and be ready. God is a generous host.

God in the World

$\mathcal{G}$od calls very ordinary people to do some extraordinary things. And they do—even children and young people. The Scriptures in this study show children or youth being called by God for special tasks or blessings. One might think they faced outstanding barriers—and they often did—but with God's help, something marvelous happened.

You may be thinking, *That was then, and this is now. My "loaf and fishes" has to feed my family, pay the bills, and put the kids through school, not take care of the whole neighborhood.* Nevertheless, we are one dynamic part of God's created order, and we are blessed with the extraordinary capability of being co-creators. We have will. We envision possibilities. We experience desire. We exhibit compassion, all on behalf of those we love or whom we come to love.

These passages invite us to examine how God woos each of us into a relationship that gives us the power to be and do our best. In so doing, we may recognize the gifts and signs God has provided to call us to a particular action at a particular time, to a vocation or lifetime work, or to a specific ministry of compassion. We are God's hands, feet, and heart at work in a battered world.

Blessing the Children

The disciples would have prevented him, but Jesus, with some indignation toward the disciples, touched and blessed the children. Children of that day were the most vulnerable of persons. Jewish children fared better than Greek and Roman children, who were the property of their fathers, even into adulthood. They had few rights as we understand them, and parents could deal very harshly with disobedient children. Showing respect to a child by confronting an adult was a pointed act of hospitality by Jesus. He blessed and empowered the powerless.

Samuel

As a child, Samuel was presented to the priests for service to the Temple. At perhaps age twelve, he heard the voice of God calling him. And after a few false starts, his priest and mentor Eli guided him in how to respond. Thus began an extraordinary and long prophetic career. Samuel's early training of service to God formed his life as a child, and then as a man, of God.

Samuel never quit on his stubborn and sinful community. We see him late in life hearing the corporate confession of a community badly in need of correction and repentance. In a profound and mature act of grace, he calls upon them to reaffirm their allegiance to the will of God and prays for them. "Far be it from me that I should sin against the LORD by ceasing to pray for you," he says (1 Samuel 12:23). But this is no "fix-it" mentality. Samuel worked and expected the people to do their part. A call to serve others demands a respect that does not give up and the courage to acknowledge one's own frailties and need for blessing.

Miriam and Others

At her mother's instruction, the young girl Miriam set her baby brother Moses afloat in the Nile River, knowing that he would attract the attention of Pharaoh's daughter. Through Miriam and her mother, this future leader and hero to Israel was saved from the threat of death that all infant Jewish males faced at this time of Jewish captivity in Egypt. Her intercession between adults (her mother and Pharaoh's daughter) united two persons whose different cultures generally offered only threat. Miriam bridged the gap, as many have done since, between strangers, cultures, and antagonists in order to accomplish the Lord's plans.

David and Goliath

As a young man, David refused to declare impossible that which God declared possible. This set a pattern for his whole life, flaws notwithstanding. David understood the importance of staying in the contest. He also understood the benefits and blessings of restraint in the face of poor hospitality, as his later dealings with Nabal show (1 Samuel 25:2-35, 39). From shepherd to king, David circulated in international and intercultural circles, always—well, usually—seeking to discern God's will in the midst of difference, turmoil, and adventure. David's story reminds us that the "battle" is the Lord's, whether actual or figurative and no matter how formidable the opposing forces.

A Boy Shares His Lunch

The disciples would have prevented him, but Jesus insisted that the hungry crowd following him be fed. In an act of extraordinary and miraculous hospitality, five loaves of barley bread and two fish fed over five thousand people. The responsibility of the host for the protection and care of his guests was made possible by a little boy's lunch. This gracious act prefigures and exemplifies the hospitality Jesus would later share with all Christians in the Lord's Supper.

Equally important, Jesus helped his disciples envision that extending hospitality on an unimaginable scale was, with his help, not only imagined but possible. God called children and youth to do extraordinary things, and with God's help, something extraordinary happened. God calls you, too.

The Stories Go On

In addition to these core passages, you will engage in studying others as well. They may seem like an eclectic array from both New and Old Testaments. We see Paul chastising the Corinthian congregation for their abuses of the fellowship meal and, in so doing, claiming the Eucharistic quality of sharing in a common meal in a sacred way. Paul also encouraged his Christian brother Philemon to welcome back Onesimus as his own brother in Christ. This slave had run away and found his way into service to the imprisoned Paul. Now Paul hoped to see him in greater service to the church. And again, Paul played a part in the conversion of Lydia, who opened her house to begin and welcome a local congregation as well as to host traveling missionaries.

In his earthly life, Jesus encountered a wealthy young man inquiring about how to inherit eternal life. In his post-resurrection life, he encountered two disciples who were wondering aloud about the completion of Jesus' earthly life.

From the Old Testament, we review the courage and wisdom of Samson's mother and his father Manoah, who welcomed an angel and received the amazing news that she would conceive a child who would begin to free the people from an enemy nation. Many centuries later, Jeremiah wrote to the nation as it languished in exile at the hands of an enemy that did conquer them—and he told the people to seek the welfare, the *shalom*, of the dominant people and land (Jeremiah 29:4-9).

The stories do not stop with the Bible. You will also get a glimpse of numerous cultural insights from San Francisco and New York's lower East Side, from the tiny island of Tonga in the Pacific, and from Calcutta, South Africa, West Africa, and Memphis, Tennessee.

God at Work in the World

What do we learn from all this? That God is at work in the world. From the earliest centuries of humankind, God has been active in the lives and hearts of God's creatures. We have lived out the story of God's love and involvement with the world. We have witnessed to the story of the God of our history. We have become the heart, hands, and feet.

We struggle to understand and to reach out to brothers and sisters in our own backyards and around the world. Sometimes we succeed and sometimes we fail, but always God calls us to reach out to the stranger, to meet and greet him or her with hospitality, and to turn that stranger into a friend. The Old Testament community obeyed this cultural practice because their lives depended on it. And in the centuries since then, the need is no less urgent.

Session One

Being Blessed

PURPOSE
The purpose of this session is to examine Jesus' blessing of the children as well as the adult "children" of God so that we become a blessing to others.

THE SESSION PLAN
Choose from among the core teaching activities and the extended session options to plan your session. **BOLD CAPS** indicate the text to which the activity relates. The icon ❖ identifies the core teaching options of the session. Add options in **Bold Italics** to extend your session beyond 45-60 minutes.

BEING BLESSED
❖ Bring a painting that you might have available, perhaps in the Sunday school supplies, of Jesus with the children. If possible,

As a child touched by Jesus—you are blessed!
—as the wind caresses the trees
—as the waves embrace the shores
—as the bird strokes the air
—as the mother cradles her child
You are blessed!
You are touched, caressed, embraced, stroked, and cradled.
You are blessed by the eternal God of us all.

_M_any Sunday school classrooms have a picture on the wall of Jesus surrounded by children as he embraces and blesses them, saying, "Let the children come to me!" It is a story remembered with fondness by many who felt in its telling their first welcome into the life of the church.

This image can continue to be a way we welcome children into the life of the church and introduce them to the "friend" they can know in Jesus. Those of us who are parents, grandparents, aunts and uncles, godparents, and

19

look for one inclusive of children from many ethnic backgrounds.

More Pictures: Post around the room as many pictures of children as you can find. Represent as many nationalities, economic situations, and cultures as possible. Invite group members to view the pictures, asking themselves to consider and answer the question: "What in this child's face reminds me of Jesus?"

❖ What is your earliest memory of hearing about Jesus? How was he described to you?

THE CHILDREN
❖ Read Mark 10:13-16. What happened? How did the disciples respond? What did Jesus do?

❖ What was the role of children in that society? What difference does it make in the way you understand your life when you see the likeness of Jesus in the face of every child?

❖ Consider this statement: "It remains true in many communities today for children to have little status.

church friends to children want them to know they belong as a significant part of the church. Congregational conversations about what it means to be a "child-friendly church" are very important.

The account of Jesus blessing the children is a wonderful way to begin our exploration of the ministry of hospitality. In this seemingly simple story, we are led into a new depth of experiencing the meaning of being a truly welcoming people in the presence of a welcoming God.

The Children

The gathering of children around Jesus might bring to mind a cluster of children brought for a story time, but the reality was much starker. A more accurate image is that of a band of street urchins curiously pushing their way forward. The adults were insulted by the presence of the children, and the disciples believed that they were irritating to Jesus. Read Mark 10:13-16.

Children in the first century had little status or honor in the society at large. While the Jewish tradition gave children rights as inheritors, Roman and Greek societies treated children as possessions. Children were likely to be seen as a burden to the household until they were of an age to help support the economy of the family. In the Jewish community, children had value by embodying "inheritance" and representing the future economic welfare of the family unit. Women

20

Children in some cultures are fed last or fed the food left over from the table where the adults, particularly the men, have gathered. Children are not allowed at the table of Communion in many communities. I have observed children pulled away from the Communion rail in order to make way for adults, who had the status and right in the culture to be first." How does this compare with your own valuation of children? What might Jesus have to say about this value (or lack of value) given to children? How does this square with what the disciples evidently thought about the presence of the children?

Status of Children: In the United States today, we often say children are given a great deal of honor and status. But current national statistics tell us that kindergarten children make up the largest group of homeless persons in the U.S. today, and the majority of those who are poor consist of children under the age of 18. What do we

were especially dependent on the birth of sons for survival in old age. A woman's wealth was measured by her children, so to be "barren" was a financial as well as a social stigma.

Jesus took advantage of the moment to teach something important to his followers. Instead of pushing the children away, as was culturally expected, Jesus reached out, drew the children close, and blessed them.

Imagine what happened to the children as a result of this embrace—gathered in, accepted, treated as a treasure, as persons of worth. Jesus was open to the children in a way that perhaps no one had been before. The children were important for who they were, not for what they represented or what they would become. Perhaps as a result of this blessing of recognition and worth, their lives were changed, even into adulthood. Were they more hospitable themselves as adults? Were they more open to persons who were seen as worthless by society? Did the children in their own families receive a blessing instead of rejection? One wonders about the impact of the blessing on these children.

Jesus consistently teaches that all people have a place in the kingdom of God. In bestowing the blessing upon the children, he bestowed power upon them as well. Jesus redefines who receives blessing and how it is received in God's community. In our time, many people experience a need for blessing as well. We may use other words: acceptance, affirmation, reassurance that we're okay.

21

believe it means to "honor" the children in light of these observations?

It could be that an experience of affirmation would serve as a doorway into the Christian life.

Embodying Hospitality

HOSPITALITY
❖ How would you rephrase these two gifts in your own words?

❖ What would it mean for you to "be a Christ for others"? Identify three or four specific examples. What would it take for you to follow through on these examples?

In the passage from Mark, there are at least two gifts presented for us to help enhance our own lives of hospitality. First, Jesus trusted the simple energy of children and the enthusiasm of their parents to experience his blessing. Jesus didn't need a complex faith statement to offer a blessing, just a personal trust. His giving was a generous act of grace that didn't stop to ask questions first. We too can risk in this way.

Second, we, like Jesus, can give our blessing to those around us. We have blessings to give that will help in healing the lives of others. Martin Luther reminded us that we can be "a Christ for others." What a great privilege we share!

Being Useful to Others

BEING USEFUL
❖ Read Paul's letter to Philemon. Using a study Bible or commentary, review the notes.

❖ What is at stake? What was a slave's standing in the Greco-Roman world?

❖ Based on what information you have and can assume, make up

A similar sense of shared blessing comes from the Letter to Philemon in the New Testament. Paul is in prison and speaks of the blessing he has received from Onesimus, a runaway slave. Paul writes to Philemon, the slave owner, inviting him to explore the possibility of a new relationship with Onesimus. Paul tells Philemon that this will be a great source of blessing to him.

In addition to these anticipated blessings, Philemon, as a slave owner and

22

the next chapter in Onesimus' history. Note the points in which God's blessing is at work for Onesimus and for the church. Then tell another story that might have occurred if Philemon had exercised his rights rather than his Christian conscience. What difference might there have been?

❖ Who are the "non-persons" in your culture, if any? In what ways do they offer a blessing to you or to the church? Have you had to change your attitude about someone as Philemon evidently did for Onesimus? What was the situation and what came about from your change? What effect has this had on your faith?

Character Study: Use a Bible dictionary or concordance to identify the persons named in this letter. Are they mentioned anywhere else in the Scriptures? If so, what does the other passage tell you about the person? What further light does that shed on your understanding of Philemon?

head of a household, had a number of rights as well. His slaves, wife, and children were essentially his property. If Onesimus had run away, he would certainly face danger upon returning home. Philemon would be within his rights to have Onesimus executed if he so chose. But Paul, in adopting this fatherly tone, encouraged Philemon to welcome Onesimus as a favored child, as a treasure to the family and to the household.

The letter does not disclose specifically what Philemon did, but tradition suggests that Onesimus became the bishop of Beroea. It does seem clear from Colossians 4:9 that Onesimus, whose name means "useful," was released from servitude to become a prominent figure in the church.

From a man with no rights, possibly even a fugitive, comes a person who serves as a blessing to the church. Paul urged Philemon to act out of love and justice rather than by right and by rules. Apparently this appeal to Philemon's Christian conscience was successful. If children and slaves—non-persons of their day—could be blessed to be a blessing, how much more might we expect of those who have power and resources to bring for the good of others? Blessings are on every side in the fellowship of Jesus Christ.

"Blessed Are You . . ."

In another of his teachings, which we call the Beatitudes (Matthew 5:1-12), Jesus gives a new context for "blessings,"

23

BLESSED ARE YOU
❖ Read Matthew 5:1-12. How does Jesus describe who is blessed and what that means? Are you blessed?

❖ These descriptors of who is blessed and why turned the popular notions of that day upside down. They probably do the same today. How would you describe these beatitudes in your own words?

❖ How much do status, inheritance, rights, good works, and so on determine social standing and expectation of success today? Would you say that this is "not the way it works with God" now, or just then? What does "work with God" mean?

Consider Transformation: In four different groups, consider the four ways transformation may be manifested (acceptance, openness, and so on). How does God call to you in these observations? What accepted norms in our own communities might Jesus want us to set aside in order to teach us more clearly

as he names the poor, the hungry, the mournful, and the suffering as those who receive a special blessing from God. This approach upset the long-accepted guidelines for who received God's special attention.

Blessings and Curses in the Scriptures

To proclaim a blessing or a curse in the Scriptures is to speak with words that are laden with power. These words are generally accompanied by gestures or symbolic actions. When a blessing is given, particularly in a gathering of persons for a religious occasion, the community is believed to be strengthened or protected through these words and actions. Similarly, curses are seen to strengthen evil forces or control them. The spoken word of blessing carries with it the power of the blessing.

Jesus is saying that the human social dependence on status, inheritance, rights, good works, good looks, or correct thinking is not how it works with God. It is the transformation of our attitudes and our lives that provides the opening into God's way of living. This transformation may be manifested in a variety of ways.

■ We may discover a new acceptance of ourselves and our gifts, as well as our shortcomings, and experience God's love and grace in our lives.

about the norms of God's community, the Kingdom of God?

Who Is Kept Out?: Think about groups or individuals who are excluded or seen as less than whole persons in society today. List as many as possible and, if you wish, then divide into small groups. Ask each group to take several of these examples and describe how you think Jesus would have responded. Use a Bible thesaurus or topical concordance to identify and examine Bible texts that relate to these examples.

■ We may find we have a new openness to people around us. It may mean a new acceptance of those whom society shuts out and shuns, whom we may have failed to understand or embrace before.

■ Those of us who are marginalized and who suffer will find that our struggle in itself provides a pathway to God's kingdom. When we hear we are "blessed," we are given a new power and identity.

■ Those of us who are affluent may find that our material possessions block the pathway to the kingdom of God, for they get in the way of spending our lives and resources for God's purposes. We may find ourselves moved to change our spending, buying, and use of resources in order to channel them into new directions.

■ If we have power and status, becoming transformed may mean using our status in a way that brings hope and change to those who have no power. We may look for ways to share power or give up long-standing privileges so others will be able to lead.

TRANSFORMED LIVES
❖ What do you think is the relationship between status, wealth, power, and blessing? What is your favorite Bible story

Transformed Lives

The Gospel stories consistently tell of persons with privilege, power, wealth, and status having to learn about a different way of living before they can follow the way of Jesus.

about transformation? What does it mean to you? Why is it important to you?

Bible Study: In groups, look up Bible stories dealing with different ways of living. What is Jesus saying through these stories? What does the main character show us about faith? How might these stories effect a transformation in you?

WEALTH

❖ Read Mark 10:17-22. What was the man asking for when he spoke with Jesus? What is surprising to you about this text? What is disturbing? What does this passage tell you about your own life? What does the writer mean by being called to be poor and faithful? Could you do this willingly? Explain.

❖ Break into small groups of four. Ask each group to discuss what they think happened to the man after he turned away from Jesus. What might you have done in his place?

■ In Mark 12:41-44 (Luke 21:1-4), we hear of the many wealthy persons who give in the Temple, but Jesus points out with praise the woman with the "mite" (a small copper coin) who gives all that she has.

■ The story of the Samaritan man in Luke 10:25-37 is an account of the disdained Samaritan being hospitable to the stranger, while the religious community members who have status and knowledge reject the stranger in need.

■ The synagogue leader Jairus (Mark 5:21-24, 35-43) has considerable status but does not use this power when he seeks out Jesus to heal his daughter. The Roman centurion, also a man of power, sought healing for his servant (Luke 7:1-10). Both had utter confidence that Jesus would and could restore their loved ones, even if their neighbors, the children of Israel, thought otherwise. They asked humbly for what they wanted, and in his grace, Jesus granted it.

Each of these stories describes a shift in power and a shift in what is "blessed" in the kingdom of God. We see in the teaching of Jesus that those whom the community has treated as the least, the deprived, and the scorned are now the chosen recipients of God's blessing. In this new configuration, those of status, wealth, and power do not automatically receive blessing. The community of peo-

26

Act Out the Story:
Ask each group to present a small skit describing the man's situation and his response to Jesus. Perhaps the skit could be a monologue, an interview with the man, or a testimony by friends and relatives about him.

Observe Your Own Power: During the week ahead, keep your senses open to and aware of certain aspects of your life that you control or dominate. These may include possessions you have or positions of authority you are given. Each day write down a phrase or sentence about the way you have experienced that day and how your possessions or position may have blocked your own experience of God. Of course, on other days these may well be means of growing in your faith. But look this week for ways in which you might simplify your life in order to follow Jesus more fully.

ple who become part of God's covenant is now much more inclusive.

Monetary and Spiritual Wealth

After the story of Jesus with the children, the Gospel of Mark follows with another story about the nature of God's blessing. We meet a wealthy man who knows and has kept the commandments. He now wants to know what he must do to receive eternal life (Mark 10:17-22). Jesus tells him he now lacks only one thing: he is to give up his possessions and to hand his money over to the poor. Jesus then calls the man to discipleship: "Then come, follow me." Shocked and grieving, the man goes away. Was he rejected by Jesus? Absolutely not, for Mark tells us that Jesus looked at him and "loved him."

The man had been a good, religious person. But in asking Jesus about eternal life, he revealed he was still searching for a deeper relationship with God. Something in him was not yet "right." Jesus saw that the man's possessions, power, and wealth were keeping him from being fully in relationship with God. Apparently Jesus was right, for the man left grieving. We do not know if he returned, but we do know that he was being called to change from rich and powerful to poor and faithful, and it was a tough choice for him to make. He had asked Jesus, in effect, for his blessing. Perhaps he felt as if he did not receive it. For those of us mature enough to understand, Jesus' blessing

27

also lays a claim on our lives for a new relationship.

Opening Our Eyes

OPENING OUR EYES

❖ How do the examples of the Celts and Mother Teresa offer a new way of seeing God at work in the world, especially through children or those who are childlike?

❖ How do you see Christ in the face of a stranger? What lessons in hospitality have you gained from the text and Scriptures?

Seeing Jesus Through the Needs of a Child: Bringing peace to the children of the world is one model for responding to Jesus' blessing of the children, as well as his call for all disciples to "become as children" in order to enter the Kingdom. In 1998, the United Nations General Assembly adopted a resolution calling for an "International Decade for a Culture of Peace and Non-Violence for the Children of the World" to be in effect from 2001 to 2010.

Centuries after Jesus blessed the children of Palestine, the people of the Celtic lands of Ireland, Wales, and Scotland embraced the tenderness of Jesus' welcome to the children in their understanding of God. Contrary to a theology developing in other parts of Christendom that focused on human sinfulness, the Celts saw in humanity—and indeed in all of creation—the goodness of God. To look deep into the eyes of a child was to see a vision of Jesus. One of the traditional blessings of children proclaimed, "The lovely likeness of the Lord is in thy pure face."

Mother Teresa of Calcutta also spoke of "seeing Jesus" in the eyes of the poorest of the poor with whom she worked. As she walked among the most destitute, the outcast, and the dying, she would look into their eyes and see the image of Jesus. When she tended to their sick bodies, she said she was bathing the body of Jesus. It was this spiritual discipline that strengthened her and enabled her to do the difficult ministry to which she was called. It was this ministry that she taught to others who came to her clinics and houses of refuge.

Children of all ages and stations find their refuge and blessing in the name of Christ. Do we remember? We are among those children welcomed into the arms of

28

This resolution coincides with the 50th anniversary of the Universal Declaration of Human Rights. Obtain a copy of the United Nations declaration from the United Nations offices in New York or through your local United Nations organization. Read this declaration and discuss how it might influence your own ministry. Consider establishing a study/action committee in your church that would look at the UN document and the United Methodist Bishop's document on Children and Poverty. Then, evaluate your church's ministry in light of these statements.

CLOSING PRAYER
❖ Close by saying the prayer together.

Jesus! We are among those children blessed and named as treasured human beings! The child in each one of us has been blessed and welcomed. We are blessed, and out of this assurance, we are able to extend that same blessing on behalf of Jesus!

It is in the open arms and welcoming, and in the face-to-face open invitation to relationship, that the way is opened into the kingdom of God. The Apostle Paul affirms in his letter to the Corinthians, "Now we see in a mirror, dimly, but then we will see face to face" (1 Corinthians 13:12). Seeing Christ face to face in the "stranger become guest," "foreigner become neighbor," and the "enemy become friend" is what the kingdom of God is all about.

Closing Prayer

Blessed Savior, you restore power to the powerless and hope to the hopeless. You set us down from high and lofty places that we might know your companionship in one another. You renew our relationships and open the closed places of our hearts. You restore our souls. Blessed be your name, now and forever. Amen.

Called by God Since Childhood

"What do you want to be when you grow up?" A child's response to this question is often long, wide ranging, and even fanciful! There can be a wonderful sense of anticipation in children as they look to what is ahead. Those children who do not have the opportunity to dream and plan are already robbed of their future. Therefore, any healthy society needs to provide room and opportunities for children to dream.

As a child, do you remember thinking about your future and what you would become? Or perhaps you had the kind of childhood where you were led more into thinking about what you were sure you did *not* want to do or be. As adults we may look back and wonder at those memories, perhaps mourning the loss of innocence or hopes gone astray. Others may look back with surprise at the ways in which our earliest inclinations led us into the adulthood we now live.

31

in half. On the left or top half, ask them to draw or list some dreams and calls they experienced in their childhood and youth. Ask them to be aware of the ways in which these were or were not calls from God. Then, on the other half of the paper, ask them to show through words or pictures the places God is calling and using them in their lives today. This may be in their work, home, church, volunteer work, or in spiritual discipline. Invite volunteers to show and explain their work.

GOD AT WORK

❖ Read Matthew 4:18-22, John 21:1-3, and Luke 8:1-3, which show Jesus' activity with others in the midst of "life things." What are the ways your own "life things" intersect with God's plans and will for you?

❖ What activities (work-related or other) engage or capture your interest? How can (or could) those activities respond to God's call and claim on your life?

God at Work in You

The subject for this session focuses on the ways in which all of us, from childhood through adulthood, can receive the message of God's call and claim on our lives. Perhaps you have not thought of your life plans as responding to God's call and claim. This session will be an opportunity to listen for the ways in which God is at work in who you are and what you do.

Sometimes we think we aren't doing what we could to respond to God's call as adults because we feel we don't have the time or energy to do the things we think are part of a faithful life. We would love to volunteer more at a homeless shelter or a hospital, spend time with reading programs for children, or work with the Boy Scouts. But the time and energy are just not there, given all of our commitments with maintaining work, home, and family. We may think our jobs are too dull and ordinary to be places where God has called us to serve.

But the Scriptures are testimony to the many ways God calls human beings in the midst of ordinary circumstances and ordinary lives. We remember the Scripture when Jesus called his disciples to leave home and work in order to follow him (Matthew 4:18-22), yet we forget that often the disciples went back to their tasks (John 21:1-3). There were also many people who, through their daily vocation, supported the ministry of Jesus by providing food, clothing, and a place to stay (Luke 8:1-3). Those who

Panel Discussion:
What are some of the moral choices our youth and children need to make in a community when some of our traditional values are being questioned? How do we help them make these choices? Invite some youth to your adult group to share some of the issues they are facing in schools and in their future. Make sure this is a time of listening to them, rather than a time of adults directing them. You might use a panel discussion format with questions supplied to a moderator (a local teacher or youth group leader, perhaps).

THE STORY OF SAMUEL
❖ Read the story of Hannah, Samuel's mother, and her visit to the Temple to pray to God (1 Samuel 1). Hannah asks for God's help, trusts in God's response, is persistent in her hope, and returns with commitment in thanksgiving. Write a prayer using these four parts of Hannah's dialogue with God. What is taking place in your life at this time for which you

are faithful and respond to the call of God are not cookie-cutter imitations of one another. They are ordinary people—just like us!

God's call comes in the midst of the complexity of human existence. God is not diverted by all the obstacles we put up in our lives. God finds a way through.

The Story of Samuel

The richly layered story of Samuel provides an intriguing peek into the history of ancient Israel and the first days of the kings of the Israelites. It is a story of responding to the call of God with faithful service in the midst of an era of upheaval and change. It provides a glimpse for us as well into our own lives.

Samuel's mother Hannah had committed him to God before his birth as part of her prayer for God to bless her with a child (1 Samuel 1). We meet Samuel in the Temple, where he serves as the assistant to the elderly priest Eli. Eli is the head of the priestly family who, through the generations from the time of the Exodus, has been given authority by God to watch over the Temple and the cultic duties. It is in this Temple that the Ark of the Covenant has been maintained. The priestly house of Eli is disintegrating because the sons of Eli have abused the privileges of the priesthood and thus sinned against God. God has promised to raise up a "faithful priest." As the priestly house of Eli is collapsing, the status and honor of young Samuel is building.

33

need to be persistently in prayer, and through which you can make a commitment of grace in return for God's provision?

Bible Characters:
Using a Bible dictionary, look up Eli, Hophni, Phineas, Elkanah, and Hannah. Skim through the portions of 1 Samuel (or elsewhere) that mention them. What do you learn about these main figures? How does this information enhance this human drama for you?

❖ At the Temple, Hannah promised that her child would belong to the Lord as long as he lived. What does it mean to "belong to the Lord"? Many of us have brought children to the church to be baptized, and we have made promises on their behalf. Discuss these baptismal vows as a group. What implications do these vows have on our own lives? on the lives of our children?

❖ Read aloud the story of Samuel's call (1 Samuel 3:1-21), with volunteers taking the parts of narrator,

The third chapter of 1 Samuel opens with a wonderful story about Samuel's call. Samuel is awakened from sleep when he hears a call from Eli, needing his help in the night. Eli denies that he called and sends Samuel back to sleep. Again the call comes, and Samuel goes to Eli. On the third occasion of the call, Eli realizes that Samuel is hearing the voice of God. He urges Samuel to listen, and the news Samuel receives is devastating: The house of Eli will be punished by the Lord for its failure to honor God.

Priestly Abuses

When the sons of Eli are accused of abusing their priestly privilege, the concern in part is their demand for their fair share of the "priest's portion" of meat from the sacrifice. They have sent their servants to get the choice cuts before the meat is boiled rather than by taking the meat with a fork from the boiling meat pot, as was the custom.

In addition, the sons of Eli have had sexual relations with the women serving in the sanctuary. This insistence by the sons to live however and to do whatever they wish is seen as a sin against God. Eli tries to correct them but is unable to control his wayward sons. God brings judgment upon the whole house of Eli because it has abused the honor of its position.

In this holy appearance, Samuel is chosen to hear and proclaim the word of

34

Samuel, the Lord, and Eli. This story is a wonderful expression of God's call. What is the central message of that call? What does it mean that "the LORD . . . let none of his words fall to the ground"?

WHEN HAVE YOU BEEN CALLED?
❖ What are some of your earliest memories of plans for your life? What is your earliest memory of God's call, and through whom did it come to you? How do you now perceive God's call and claim on your life?

❖ Children and youth today face situations and decisions that many adults have not had to face. In what ways can you provide support to them in these difficult times? How can you help them see the work and love of God in the midst of their own lives, experiences, and activities?

the Lord, in a time when "the word of the LORD was rare" (1 Samuel 3:1). From the time of his call, Samuel continues to grow and learn in the midst of the disintegrating priestly house. We learn that "as Samuel grew up, the LORD was with him and let none of his words fall to the ground" (1 Samuel 3:19). Samuel is true and faithful and becomes known as the prophet who speaks for God.

When Have You Been Called?

Samuel's call came when he was about 12 years of age. I remember my own call at age 12, when I experienced the inexplicable presence of God as the bishop's hand was laid on my head for my confirmation.

My husband knew encouragement and belonging through the listening ear of a Sunday school teacher and a congregation that invited him at 11 years old to play the organ. At 12, my son is clear that he will be a writer and has already begun his work.

It is no accident that the Jewish synagogue brings children into full membership at 13 by bar or bat mitzvah, and many churches arrange for confirmation classes at this same age. It is the time when we begin to separate ourselves from family and begin to learn new ways of relating to others. It is also an important time to claim a relationship with God.

Perhaps you didn't then name it as a call from God, but over the years you have come to understand it in that way. God has indeed guided each of us from our earliest years and stayed with us to teach and lead us through the choices of our lives.

In the same way, we are reminded that God calls and works through youth and children in our community this very day—sometimes in the midst of painful tragedy, such as the shooting deaths in recent years of students and teachers in several schools. Young people have dreams and hopes, and God touches their lives. Some will be led to speak out, to work for peace, to bring new understanding in their schools, and to make a difference in other arenas of life. Children and youth are responding to the nudges of God in their lives and are seeking some answers and direction for their future. Perhaps you can name examples in your own community of youth who are speaking out for the things they believe are right.

Eli Guides Samuel

ELI GUIDES SAMUEL
❖ Skim through 1 Samuel 2–4 to remind yourselves of what we know about Eli. How did Eli interact with Samuel? What did he offer and what did he receive in this relationship? Think again about how God was at work here.

Samuel was called by God to serve, and God watched over him in his growing role as prophet. When God calls us to service, God always supports our growth and education beyond the initial beckoning and urging so that we learn how to do God's will and become the kind of people God is leading us to become. Perhaps some of us have not really trusted this promise of God's ongoing presence and will especially need to absorb the Samuel story.

36

❖ List some of the opportunities you have in your church to be "elders" to the children and youth in your midst. Who was an "elder" for you and what effect did it have on your life? What can adult leaders do to keep hope and vision alive in our children and youth as they face the future?

Pray: for a youth or child whom you know, perhaps from outside your family, daily during the week ahead.

Providing Guides: What is your church doing to provide guides and "elders" for the children and youth in your church and wider community? Many confirmation programs now provide an opportunity for an adult to mentor a youth during this time of learning and decision making. Perhaps this is a role you might consider. Or perhaps there are other ways to establish connections with children and youth either together or individually. This kind of outreach may not require a lot of your time but rather

Our children and youth particularly need to know that they have special gifts given by God and that God will help them use these gifts in the best way possible. One of our tasks as their elders, whether through parenting or other relationships, is to guide children and youth in directions that will help them fully blossom into what God intended. The priest Eli did this for Samuel. He helped Samuel understand God's call by helping him to discern God's voice. He guided Samuel to listen to the word of God. Then he helped Samuel to give voice and meaning to the words that God had brought. Finally Eli "let go" of Samuel, "loosing the apron strings" and releasing Samuel to fulfill God's unfolding plans for him.

In our guidance of children and youth, we may be aware of our own shortcomings and failures. Perhaps we can take solace in the figure of Eli. Much of what he and his forebears had built was falling to pieces. The old systems and relationships were dying out, and Eli had failed profoundly with his own sons. But in Samuel he found a son of his own heart and was able to provide the most important guidance in Samuel's life: the ability to hear, see, and respond to God.

This compels each of us to be open to the calling of "guiding elder" to the children and youth in our midst. We may be aware of our own limitations and failures, and our house may seem to be falling apart, but the Almighty God has a way of using us even in our most weakened state to bring about God's good word and God's good kingdom.

The Implications of Samuel's Call for Our Time

It is tempting to stop here, but the facts of the story of Samuel compel us to dig deeper. Samuel's call came in a time of crisis and change. The authority of Temple and religious tradition had come under profound scrutiny. God's judgment was placed upon the priests of the Temple for their failure to honor God and their abuse of privileges as priests. The sons of Eli, Hophni and Phinehas, chose a moral course that led to their destruction (1 Samuel 2:34).

We may need to listen carefully to this aspect of the story, for in it we hear that when we serve God, we are under God's grace and affirmation as well as under God's judgment. Our privileged relationship with God requires a mutual covenant or promise that we will not abuse the gifts God has given us. There is a profound responsibility and a huge blessing for those who understand themselves to be servants of God. We are reminded that we are responsible for our actions and decisions. We must ask ourselves, one another, our communities, our children and youth, our government, and our elected leaders, "Are we making decisions that build up or that destroy? What kind of future are we willing to live with?"

Send Us a King

Samuel lived as a judge and prophet in the midst of the people, guiding them in

your willingness to be present at times to listen and help interpret the voices that come to our youth "in the night."

IMPLICATIONS

❖ What does it mean to you to "be under God's grace and affirmation as well as under God's judgment"? What are the implications of being in a "privileged relationship with God [that] requires a mutual covenant or promise that we will not abuse the gifts God has given us"?

❖ What are the decisions that we make as a church, community, or nation that build up? that destroy? What decisions have you made as an individual that build up? that destroy? What has been the effect of those decisions?

SEND US A KING
❖ Read 1 Samuel 9–10 for an introduction to Saul.

Saul and Kingship: Using a Bible commentary or dictionary, find a more complete portrait of Saul and of the implications of asking for a king.

the way of the Lord. It was a time of political upheaval, as the Israelites faced the threat of the mighty armed force of the coastal Philistines. The tension with the Philistines mounted, and the people began to clamor for a king to lead them. Finally, the Lord told Samuel that they needed a ruler to help save them from the Philistines. In a vision the Lord came to Samuel and told him: "I will send to you a man from the land of Benjamin, and you shall anoint him to be ruler over my people Israel. He shall save my people from the hand of the Philistines; for I have seen the suffering of my people . . ." (1 Samuel 9:16). This king was a young man named Saul, whom Samuel had anointed (1 Samuel 10:1).

Samuel's Farewell Address

SAMUEL'S FAREWELL
❖ Read 1 Samuel 12. Review the historical highlights of Samuel's address. What was the interrelationship between Samuel, God, and the community?

❖ How did the people respond to Samuel's address? What was the nature of their sin? For them, what were the "useless things that cannot profit or save"? What are the things for you that you need to put aside?

When Samuel neared the end of his life, he gave a final speech (1 Samuel 12), reminding the people of the work he had done with the Lord's help and asking for confirmation that he had done his work fairly and honestly. He reminded them of the history of God's ongoing commitment to the people of Israel. We see in this speech the interrelationship between Samuel, God, and the people. Samuel did not do his work alone and of his own will, but in commitment to God and in commitment to the community.

Samuel's whole life was dedicated to God. His mother had prayed for him even before his conception and then gave him to God. He was taken to the Temple as a

24-Hour Clock:
Prepare a "24-hour clock" for each person. (Make a large circle with numbers around the edges, 1-24. On the clock hands, secured with a paper fastener or brad, write the text "Serve the Lord with all your heart.") Invite participants to use this "clock" as a spiritual discipline in the coming week, noting on the clock face the time they felt they have spent on "useless things" and also activities and attitudes that do serve God. Save time in the next session to talk about the experience.

toddler and raised by the priest to be a priest and prophet. God's power and word were with him so strongly and obviously that even from childhood, Samuel was recognized as someone very devout and special.

It is no surprise that as an adult, he served such a potent and faithful role with the people, holding them accountable to the same criteria of faithfulness by which he lived. Samuel urged the community not to turn aside from following the Lord, but to "serve the LORD with all your heart; and do not turn aside after useless things that cannot profit or save . . ." (1 Samuel 12:20-21).

This urgent call to service was also a reminder that Israel was a theocracy—that is, a community ruled by God. Even asking for a king was a breach of faith, yet God had acquiesced and provided a king. Still, the people were to recognize and acknowledge that any temporal leader, including Samuel and Saul, was the agent of God's leadership.

The community easily forgot this lesson and frequently turned to other nations or foreign gods. Samuel reminded the people that there was always the price of judgment for turning away, including the risk that God would turn away from them or allow them to fall into the hands of their enemies. Nevertheless, he assured them of God's continuing regard. In the same way, Samuel committed himself to unceasing prayer for the people, asking them to remember all the great things that God had done.

The Ongoing Story

THE ONGOING STORY

❖ One description of the task of God's people is to be "bridge builders," connecting people across their differences with one another, and connecting people to the way of God as Samuel did. Draw a bridge on a sheet of paper posted on the wall. Brainstorm some of the ways you are already building bridges in your daily lives. Then name some of the potential sources of bridge building.

❖ How is Samuel's example an inspiration or challenge to you?

The story of Samuel marks a pivotal change in the life of the people of Israel as they move from independent tribes and clans to a united monarchy under one king. It is a tale of transition as the people move from old systems of social structure and authority to new systems and understandings of what it means to be the people of God. Samuel served to remind them of their past and helped to guide them into the future.

The Birth of a Nation

At the beginning of the book of First Samuel, Israel is a loose federation of tribal groups experiencing both an external and internal crisis that threatens its existence. By the end of Second Samuel, Israel has developed into a nation-state and has formed a hereditary monarchy. Israel is transformed socially and politically, from agrarian tribal existence into complex economic systems based on trade and the accumulation of wealth, from independence to centralized political systems. These changes influence the systems of the religious life of the Israelites.

Samuel served to bridge the gap between the need of the people and the plan of God. He is seen speaking for both

41

the people and for God. The story reminds us to be faithful to our commitment to the work and tasks to which we are called. It likewise nudges us to realize that God will lead us to people and places we did not know would have such a profound effect on our lives. We learn that God will judge reckless disregard for the commitments we make, and at the same time God will work with us in our perceived needs—and even demands—in order to preserve us as a faithful people.

A Society in Transition

A SOCIETY IN TRANSITION

❖ How do you see the world in a time of crisis and change as we enter the 21st century?

❖ What are some of the changes that do or could call into question the existence of the church? As a person of faith, how would you address those challenges, and what influence or impact do they have on you?

As we enter into the 21st century, we are aware of discussions which speak of a "paradigm shift" in the way we perceive reality. There are so many changes, with new assumptions in operation, that the very paradigm, or framework, through which we operate in the world is changing. The shift might be described as a kaleidoscope in which the whole arrangement of the colors is constantly shifting and being altered. These shifts take place in the economy, in science and medicine, and in political and communication systems. Some have compared the change into the world of computers and Internet communication as a shift comparable to the building of the printing press. The church is involved in examination of its own structures, systems, and assumptions as it faces changes in society that call the church's very existence into question. As people of faith, we need to explore new dimensions of God's call into our lives to engage the paradigm shift.

"Only Fear the LORD"

"ONLY FEAR THE LORD"

❖ What insights from the session help you understand what it means to be in service to God? in mission to others?

❖ What would it mean for you to become more concerned with finding ways to give God's grace, which you have received, back into the service of God?

❖ Close with prayer for all those in service to God.

"Only fear the LORD, and serve him faithfully with all your heart" (1 Samuel 12:24) is the guidance finally given by Samuel. To be in mission is to open our hearts and serve faithfully as God calls us to do so. To follow Samuel as a model for what it means to be in mission is to seek to bridge the gap between God and the people, between God's plan and the people's needs. Our daily lives certainly present many opportunities for this kind of service in the name of God.

Session Three

The Right Place and the Right Time

PURPOSE
The purpose of this session is to recognize the places where God is at work and the ways in which we can serve God wherever we are.

THE SESSION PLAN
Choose from among the core teaching activities and the extended session options to plan your session. **BOLD CAPS** indicate the text to which the activity relates. The icon ❖ identifies the core teaching options of the session. Add options in **Bold Italics** to extend your session beyond 45-60 minutes.

THE RIGHT PLACE
❖ Do you agree with Archbishop Tutu about experiencing what it means to be really human? What benefit do you see in cross-

$\mathcal{A}$ number of years ago, a journalist asked Archbishop Desmond Tutu of South Africa what he would do with a sudden gift of a large amount of money. Archbishop Tutu spoke of many needs and many projects, and then he said, "I would keep some of my funds to help get people out of the claustrophobic atmosphere of South Africa—get them to meet other people in different parts of the world so that they could experience what it means to be really human. It is a liberating experience." In the midst of the oppression of a closed and confining system, there was a need to encounter the stranger in order to enable black South Africans again to hear their full name: "Child of God."

The ordinary image of a stranger is one who has need of something we can give—whether it is someone in distress in the parking lot of the grocery store or the stranger far away in need of emergency relief funds. Yet, as Archbishop Tutu's comment demonstrates, we have need of the stranger just as much as the

45

cultural experiences and exchanges? What harm, if any?

❖ When have you met a stranger who has influenced your life for the good? Do you agree that a stranger is necessarily someone who needs something? Do we need the stranger to give us our name? Explain.

THE STRANGER
❖ What stories do you recall, from the Bible or other sources, of the mysterious stranger who has the power of transformation on those whom he or she encounters? Do you agree with Palmer that the stranger is a key figure in public life? Explain.

❖ Have you ever had the experience of being in a strange place and learning something new and important about yourself? How might your life have been different were it not for that experience?

stranger needs us, in order to restore our full humanity—robbed by oppression, by prejudice and bigotry, by violence, by an environment that tells us that some persons have more worth than others. We need the stranger to remind us who we are and what we are meant to do and be. We need the stranger to give us our name. This is one of the powerful dimensions of the biblical witness that tells of the role of the stranger in our midst.

The Stranger

In his book *The Company of Strangers* (Crossroad, 1985), Parker Palmer speaks about the importance of our public life, lived beyond the private realm, as the place in which we experience "the fullness of God's word for our lives." He says, "The key figure in public life is the stranger. The stranger is also a central figure in biblical stories of faith, and for good reason. The religious quest, the spiritual pilgrimage, is always taking us into new lands where we are strange to others and they are strange to us. . . . The very idea of faith suggests a movement away from our earthly securities into the distant, the unsettling, the strange. Even if we stay at home . . . the stranger who comes into our lives may well be a pilgrim bearing news."

The biblical encounters we experience in this session of our study help us explore strangers suddenly appearing and influencing the direction of our lives.

It is about being in the right place at the right time and claiming the moment.

The Mother, the Daughter, and the Princess

Read Exodus 2:1-10. Miriam is not a well-known figure in the biblical story, but she carries out a significant role for the Hebrew people. She was the older sister of Moses, and it was she who delivered him into the rushes, in his woven basket, in order to save his life. She protected him from the campaign of infanticide being carried out by the Egyptian Pharaoh against the Israelites. Miriam hid in the plants at the water's edge and watched Pharaoh's daughter as she discovered Moses and then took him as her own child. Miriam came out of hiding, offering to find a wet nurse for the infant, who in fact was the mother of Moses and Miriam. Through the years Miriam stayed connected with Moses and became a prophet among her people.

The story of Miriam and Moses is a curious one. Miriam has the critical role as one who intervenes between two enemies and enables compassion and reconciliation. We are familiar with the story of Moses, but perhaps we need to reread it with "new eyes." What we see may shock us. We are certainly amazed by the willingness of the mother to trust her child to the risks of the open river, and even more amazed by the willingness of the Pharaoh's daughter to bring into her care a Hebrew male child, whom her own

MOTHER, DAUGHTER, PRINCESS
❖ Read Exodus 1:1–2:10 for an overview of the circumstances in Egypt into which Moses was born. Who are the key characters who work for the preservation of the Israelites? who work against them?

Read Exodus 15:20-21: One of the oldest portions of Scripture is the text ascribed here to Miriam, a song that speaks of the triumph of the Israelites' escape from Egypt. Look up Miriam in a Bible dictionary for more information on her life and character.

❖ At the time of Moses' birth, although Miriam was not yet an adult, still she played a crucial role of intervention or intercession. Do you know any young people who have intervened in risky situations for the greater good? What happened? What motivated them to do what they did? What effect did their actions have?

47

❖ What does it mean to you to claim life in the face of something that threatens to destroy? What divisions of culture, religion, class, and political systems clash and work against life and wholeness for all persons? How do you see God at work in this story? in your own story?

Consider the Other Women: Refer again to Exodus 1:15-22. Shiprah and Puah played a special role in the salvation of Moses and other male babies. Research this passage in a Bible commentary. What did the women do? At what risk?

MIRIAM PRINCIPLES
❖ Divide into four small groups. Ask each group to discuss one of the "Miriam Principles."

father was seeking to kill! We are struck as well with the tale of the mother, who gives up her child for safety and then receives him again to nurture until he is "grown" and is ready to carry out his calling.

These three remarkable women worked together in extraordinary ways to enable the events of God's history to unfold. They were willing to take risks and to reach across the divisions of culture, religion, class, and political systems in order to cooperate for a greater purpose. They sought to be faithful to what they thought was right in the midst of the circumstances in their lives.

What more can any of us do than this—to be faithful in the face of what we experience in the realities of our lives. Some would say that God tests us by giving us difficult circumstances to overcome. Others would say instead that God does not so much give us the difficult circumstances, but rather requires us, if we are faithful to our heritage as God's people, to claim life in the face of that which threatens to destroy us. These three women—Moses' mother, Miriam, and the Pharaoh's daughter—worked against destruction, took risks in the face of danger, and cooperated with one another across deep divisions.

The "Miriam Principles"

God calls to us in just these kinds of circumstances. We are called to live out the "Miriam Principles" as God's faithful people:

■ to protect from danger the precious and innocent in our midst;

■ to find connections among communities to enable the safety of the threatened;

■ to use our power and status for the good of those who are at risk;

■ to find God's will for reconciliation and restoration in the political reality of the time.

These are not easy tasks, yet at the same time they are tasks that can be realistically undertaken within the realm of our own daily lives.

Another Remarkable Woman

In another story of faith in the face of difficulty, we meet Manoah's wife, a nameless yet bright and courageous woman and the mother of Samson. We read about Manoah and his wife before Samson's birth while they were living in the foothills between Dan and Judah. One day an angel of the Lord appeared to Manoah's wife and announced to her that she was no longer barren and would have a son, who would "begin to deliver Israel from the hand of the Philistines" (Judges 13:5). He told her to avoid wine and unclean food and that her son would be part of the nazirite community, people who took special vows of consecration before God. She reported to her husband that she had met a "man of God

49

his wife. What happens to you when you feel that you have seen the face of God?

❖ Samson's mother is never given a name in the Scriptures, yet she is faithful and central to the story. At what other times are you aware of persons going "nameless" yet being instrumental in making a difference in the community?

Barren Women: A frequent motif in the hero stories of the Bible is the birth of a male child to a woman previously barren. The birth is not only a blessing to the woman but has even greater implications for the wider community. Look up "barrenness" in a Bible dictionary, such as *The Interpreter's Dictionary of the Bible* (Abingdon), or "child, children." What other women were barren until God intervened? What happened to their children?

ANOINTED, CHOSEN, FLAWED
❖ Read Judges 14–16 to learn about Samson's life and adventures. What seemed to be his best

. . . [whose] appearance was like that of an angel" (Judges 13:6).

Manoah entreated God to send the man again, that he might hear for himself the news and understand it. The Lord apparently agreed to this request for a sign and again sent the messenger. Manoah was full of questions: What was the meaning and what were the consequences of his news, and just who was this messenger anyway? He was told the messenger's name was "too wonderful." The stranger was invited to a meal, which became instead a sacrificial offering, and the angelic messenger disappeared in the flame of the altar.

It was then that Manoah realized that the stranger was an angel from God, and he became very frightened. Manoah's wife saw and experienced an anointing by God in the stranger's presence. Samson was born, and as he grew, "the LORD blessed him. The spirit of the LORD began to stir him . . ." (Judges 13:24-25). Each of these persons was faithful first. They rose to the situations in which they found themselves and took initiative to continue. They are a model of faithfulness, though not without flaws, for the community of believers.

Anointed, Chosen, and Full of Flaws

The story of Samson is a relief for us ordinary folks, for it confirms that things can go wrong even among those whom and worst characteristics? What about his relationship with God? with the Hebrews? What kind of role model does he present to you? Can you relate to his life at all? If so, how? What does Samson teach you about faith and about taking responsibility for exercising your gifts from God for God?

The Philistines: Research in a Bible dictionary who the Philistines were, where they came from, and their contentious relationship with Israel.

❖ The role of women in the Samson story seems to represent the disintegration of the whole people of Israel. After the initial story of Samson's mother, women are presented in a negative way. They are caught in the powers of a male-dominated society. For more commentary on this, see *The New Interpreter's Bible,* Volume II, page 860.

Flawed Leaders: There has been much news about the flawed behavior of world leaders, as well as conversation about the impact

God has especially blessed. Perhaps we can make a difference after all, even though things so often go wrong with us, too! It tells us as well of the coming of strangers who can lead us to fulfillment or lead us far astray.

Samson is the last of the judges in the Hebrew tradition (he predates Eli and Samuel). His story reflects many aspects of the lives of the great judges, but in contrast, where they succeeded, he seemed to fail. He lived at a time when the Philistines were a major political threat to the tribes of Israel. The Philistines were people who had come from the Aegean and from Asia Minor and settled in the coastal area of Canaan about the 12th century B.C. The conflict with the Philistines continued on through the stories of King Saul and King David.

While the other judges of Israel acted on behalf of the whole of Israel, Samson seemed to act only for himself. He was enamored with women, and his romantic escapades were the source of much of his trouble. He first married a Philistine woman, who tricked him and exposed him to danger. His repeated relationships put him in peril and the Israelite people as well. His final love was Delilah, who tricked him into telling her the source of his power—his uncut hair. Of course, it was not the hair itself, but the symbol of consecrated vows as a nazirite that his uncut hair repre-sented. The Philistines cut off his hair in his sleep, and "his strength left him. . . . He did not know that the LORD had left him" (Judges 16:19-20). His final act was to pray to God to restore his strength so that of the private actions and the public deeds of politicians. What do we learn about these issues through the Samson story? Where is God's word of judgement? Where is God's word of grace?

RELENTLESS LOVE

❖ Would you describe Samson as both a tragic and comic figure? If so, why? Do you see God's relentless love in this story? If so, where and how?

❖ In what tragic and comic events in your own life have you seen God at work? What effect has this had on your own sense of mission and dedication to God?

The Spirit of the Lord: Provide some meditative music, along with water colors and paper. Ask participants to spend some time in free flow painting depicting the movement of the Spirit of the Lord. Encourage them to set aside their adult need to make an artistic work, and instead paint with their feelings. If you can lower the lighting in the room, do so.

he might bring down the household that contained "all the lords of the Philistines" (Judges 16:27). His last desire was granted, and they all died together, "so those he killed at his death were more than those he had killed during his life" (Judges 16:30).

Relentless Love

Samson is both a tragic and comic figure, yet he provides a completely different picture of God's consecrated people than we have had before. He fails, he is led astray, his love life gets in his way, and he does not accomplish all that he could have. But his remarkable trait is his enduring love and loyalty. He is constantly disappointed and betrayed by those he loves—women and troops both—yet that does not stop his love and commitment. He breaks his covenant with God repeatedly (by eating unclean food, killing for personal revenge, touching a corpse, marrying a Philistine). Still, God continues to make use of him despite his flaws and failures. It is God who triumphs in the story, not the potential hero Samson. The spirit of the Lord continues to rush upon Samson, and God's purposes are fulfilled. *The New Interpreter's Bible* , Volume II (Abingdon, 1998, p. 862) observes: "The Samson story affirms God's willingness to enter into the full sinfulness and rebellion of humankind in order to accomplish the purposes of God in the world. . . . The figure of Samson embodies . . . God's amazing and relentless love. God keeps coming back to God's sinful people, responding to their cries of distress and promising to stay with them in and through their failures, their captivities, their exiles, and even their deaths."

We have been warned that we might be "entertaining angels unawares" when we meet the stranger, but repeatedly the Scriptures tell us of the many times the holy is in our midst and we do not recognize it at all. Popular culture has romanticized the idea of angels, and popular bookshelves are full of stories, not to mention films and TV shows. But the angels of biblical tradition are not always comforting, are often unfamiliar, and even wrestle with us in the wilderness places of our lives.

Strangers into Friends

We often encounter God's presence in unexpected places and through unexpected people. There was a large group of people in a village in West Africa who were eager to establish a church. They had very little money and couldn't afford to build. They needed a place to meet, sheltered from the rains and the heat of the day. A woman in the village who was a leader and paramount chief heard of their need, and she decided it was important that the church be established in their village. She offered the substantial porch of her house and the grounds of her compound so that the people might gather for prayers and singing and so that a church could be established.

STRANGERS INTO FRIENDS
❖ What does the story about the new church teach you about hospitality? If the situation were reversed, do you think that a Christian chief would have extended the same courtesy to a Muslim group? Explain. Is it possible for interreligious groups to be "friends" here? Is it appropriate? If so, to what extent? Explain your response.

53

The woman did not join the church, for she felt no need. She believed in God, whom she called Allah, and continued to follow the important religious traditions of her Muslim faith. Among these traditions is that of honoring all people "of the Book"—Christians, Jews, and Muslims together. And a new United Methodist Church was established in the village because of the generosity of this "stranger" to the Christian faith.

The book of Acts tells of the emergence of the church and the travels of Paul throughout many nations to spread the gospel. We find Paul, in the middle of the first century, near the modern region of Macedonia, where in early 1999 refugees were fleeing from the war of Kosovo. Paul is preaching at a riverside in Philippi with Timothy on a Sabbath day, joining people who had gathered for prayer. It is not a synagogue, for those present are probably not Jews but are "worshipers of God." One of the listeners is a woman named Lydia, a dealer in purple cloth from the city of Thyatira. (Purple cloth was worn only by the elite class, which would indicate that Lydia was an accomplished and wealthy businesswoman.)

The Scriptures report that "the Lord opened her heart to listen eagerly to what was said by Paul" (Acts 16:14). She did not know him and had simply come to the riverside that day for prayers, as was her custom. But in the words of this passing stranger, God touched her heart in a new way. She responded to him by inviting Paul and Timothy to stay in her

❖ Read Acts 16:11-15. Note that after being released later from prison, Paul and Silas returned to Lydia's home (16:40). What do you learn about Lydia? What lessons in hospitality to you see demonstrated?

❖ Traveling missionaries depended on the openness of Christian homes in the regions they visited. Why do you think this was this so? How are your home and attitude hospitable?

More About Lydia:
Look up Lydia in a Bible dictionary or a commentary on Acts. What is a "worshiper of God"? What is the significance of the purple cloth? What does it mean that a woman was a dealer in purple cloth?

home, which they would presumably make the center point of their ministry. Her whole household was baptized, and she most likely became the leader and economic support of the church in the region (Acts 16:40).

Lydia came along to the right place at the right time to hear strangers who changed the course of her life. Paul and Timothy met the stranger Lydia and received hospitality in her home, as well as the affirmation of a ministry well done. She became a friend to them and a model of hospitality.

Befriending Strangers

BEFRIEND STRANGERS

❖ How does the writer feel she had been in the right place at the right time in receiving the request from the delegation? Do you believe their request to deliver these letters was a reasonable one? Would you have accepted the call? Explain. What are you willing to do for a stranger in your community?

In early 1980, hostages were taken in Iran as part of the ongoing conflict between the United States and that nation, which became known as the "Tehran Hostage Crisis." I received a phone call one day from a representative of the National Council of Churches, who had just returned from a visit to the hostages. The delegation had brought back letters and was looking for clergy in every community across the United States where the hostages' families lived to deliver the letters. It was an extraordinary opportunity to reach out in ministry to strangers, including the ambassador's family. We brought them words of hope and encouragement by carrying letters that reconnected them with the ones they loved. It was not a ministry I sought out nor expected, but I was simply available, in the right place at the right time, and was open to the call.

55

FRIENDS AND "ENEMIES"

❖ How do you define "enemy"? Do you have enemies? If so, who? What are the barriers that separate you? How could you be like Pharaoh's daughter and reach over those barriers? Would you want to? What if God called you to do so? How would you know God's wishes for you?

Watch a Video: Obtain a video dealing with some aspect of the Civil Rights Movement, such as *Four Little Girls* by Spike Lee, or the PBS documentary *Eyes on the Prize.* Arrange a time to show the film and discuss it together. Be sure to have the proper license for a group showing.

❖ Read the anecdote about Rev. Lawson and his son. How would you address his musings? his reaction to the rejection and anger? Have you had any personal experience with segregation and rejection (on either side)? Does the kind of experience Rev. Lawson describes remind you of incidents in your own life?

This is exactly what it means to be present to the urging and callings of God in our life, to reach out to the stranger and bring some measure of restoration to both their and our lives.

Friends and "Enemies"

Hospitality among strangers can also become a means of breaking down barriers that keep people separated from one another. We saw this generosity of spirit in the Pharaoh's daughter as she lifted the foreign child from the Nile, in direct defiance of her father's order of genocide. Miriam, even as a child, interjected herself between the power of destruction (Pharaoh's orders) and the power of life (her mother, nursing the infant Moses). Jesus modeled this in his own ministry as he socialized with those outside of his social standing.

During the struggling days of the Civil Rights movement, Rev. James M. Lawson, Jr., one of the critical leaders of the movement, looked for opportunities for strangers to become neighbors and for enemies to become friends. He was the primary leader in the nonviolent stance of the movement and trained many people in nonviolence.

When he was in Memphis, Tennessee, he would take his young son John to the park every day to play. Often a sign would be posted on the gate of the park by the Memphis zoo: "No colored people allowed in the zoo today." And each day Rev. Lawson simply walked past the sign

❖ What kind of damage might be done "on both sides of the racial ledger" when we refuse to see past prejudice? refuse to offer appropriate hospitality? rely on stereotypes or fears rather than love for others?

CLOSING

❖ Ask each member of the group in the week ahead to commit to praying for a stranger they may encounter—perhaps someone they see daily but do not know, or a stranger who happens by on the street. Keep this person, even if you do not know him or her by name, in your prayers and in your heart all week long.

❖ Then pray together: Risen Christ, who enters into locked hearts with the key of compassion and care, help us to follow you that our hearts may stay open to the stranger and the enemy. Help us be welcoming to those who would disturb our safe and protected existence, that we might fully know unity with all your creation. Amen.

and took in his child to play. Some days were uneventful, and young John would play happily with the other children, the only black child in their midst. But on other days, as the children would play, one parent would suddenly notice what had happened. Storming into the play yard, the irate parent would pull her own child away from the activity, with words of admonition that he "never do that again."

It disturbed Rev. Lawson, not for his own child, who he said was of strong character and knew who he was and that he was loved, but for the other children. *"Did, Lawson wondered, the white child come away with some inner sense that the problem was him? Perhaps the white kids would think they were not good enough, or worthy enough, or strong enough to play with this black child.* Damage, he became more convinced than ever before, was being done on both sides of the racial ledger" (David Halberstam, *The Children*, Random House, 1998).

One wonders as the years went by if the parents or the children remembered these incidents, and if they came to see them as lost opportunities for community, as lost chances to meet an angel "unawares" and to find in the stranger a fuller understanding of who they really are.

Session Four

Up Against Giants

PURPOSE
The purpose of this session is to gain greater insight into understanding hospitality and overcoming barriers that might prevent participation in one's personal calling.

THE SESSION PLAN
Choose from among the core teaching activities and the extended session options to plan your session. **BOLD CAPS** indicate the text to which the activity relates. The icon ❖ identifies the core teaching options of the session. Add options in **Bold Italics** to extend your session beyond 45-60 minutes.

UP AGAINST GIANTS
❖ Prepare for this session by reading 1 Samuel 17 and 1 Samuel 25:2 42.

The contemporary world is interconnected in extraordinary and complicated ways, through the Internet and e-mail, telecommunication systems, financial ventures, and corporate mergers. Perhaps technology has brought the world much closer together than we are yet prepared to manage. As small as the world has become, those things that we felt we could manage and influence have grown so large that we seem to be up against a giant, with very little being within our ability to control.

Even with instant communication now possible around the world, the most important communication—that which helps us understand and respect one another—is undeveloped. We don't understand each other's languages and cultures. We don't appreciate one another's traditions and experiences. Stories of ethnic cleansing, occurrences of racism, and accounts of religious oppression fill the news. All of these remind us we have a long way to go to be a global community. We struggle to

59

understand what it means to be socially responsible adults and faithful Christians when we cannot understand the complexity of the global economy. We are embarrassed that we cannot name, or place on a map, the nations mentioned in the nightly news. We wonder how we can possibly be people of hospitality to our own community, let alone the rest of the world!

FACING THE GIANT
❖ Review 1 Samuel 17. What is going on here? What is David's ultimate point that rallies the Israelites? How can God be present when "Davids and Goliaths" meet one another?

❖ Form two groups. Name one side Goliath and the other David. Ask each side to meet in their own group and talk about what it means to be the character they are (for example, what it is like to be powerful and well armored, what it is like to be vulnerable and seen as weak, what it feels like to have the tables turned). Ask each group to report back to the other and then discuss the experience together.

Facing Up to the Giant

The theme of giants and monsters seems appropriate as we face the gigantic and monstrous issues of our time. The Old Testament has its "giant" story as well, about David, the shepherd boy, who comes up against Goliath the giant and slays him with only a stone and a slingshot. The boy triumphs over the giant, little conquers large, an oppressor meets his match in a vulnerable boy, and good triumphs over evil.

The story is set in the midst of ongoing armed conflict between the Philistines and the Israelites. The Philistines lived along the coastal areas, where Tel Aviv and the Gaza Strip are located today. The Philistines had gathered on one mountain, the Israelites on the other, and they were separated by a valley. The Philistines sent a huge man named Goliath into the valley to challenge the Israelites. He measured about 6 feet 9 inches tall and was covered head to toe with armor and bronze. His sword was of bronze as well, and his spear had

60

Theologize: The biblical story tells of Goliath's beheading, but the theological message might actually imply another kind of ending to the story. Retell the conclusion of the story to explore those theological implications.

an iron tip. Iron smelting was a new technology in that era, and apparently the Philistines had the monopoly on this skill and industry. These metals were mentioned to point out their superiority over the materials from which the Israelites' weapons were crafted.

Goliath wanted the Israelites to send a man to fight him face to face and promised that the winner would be named victor of the war. The challenge produced great fear among the Israelites, and the situation grew very tense, with Goliath engaging in daily psychological warfare, challenging them from the valley for 40 days in a row. At this point the shepherd boy David arrived at the battle scene. He heard Goliath's taunts and watched the Israelites flee in fear. David challenged them: "Who is this uncircumcised Philistine that he should defy the armies of the living God?" (1 Samuel 17:26). His older brother was angered by David's presence, but King Saul took the boy seriously. David announced to the king that he wished to fight Goliath and insisted he was able because of his experience defending the sheep.

Saul gave his blessing and dressed David for battle, but David found the armor and weapons ill fitting, overweight, and confining. He removed them and simply took his shepherd's staff, five smooth stones, and his sling to face the giant. In the name of the Lord of hosts, David, armed with sling and stone, struck the Philistine in the one vulnerable place in his armor—the middle of his forehead—and Goliath fell. David beheaded the giant, and the victory for Israel was the Lord's! Thus began the rise of David, the great King of Israel.

Facing Our Own Giants, Within and Without

The story of David and Goliath may seem strange given our theme of "Hospitality and Mission." Somehow a beheading does not seem very hospitable! One wonders how stories of facing giants can be peaceful. But there are some intriguing points to this story that point us toward an understanding of mission.

Giants are deceptive; a giant is only as large as we are small! When we look at issues of concern to us as faithful people—world hunger, poverty, the gap between rich and poor, nuclear warfare—we can feel very tiny indeed. We may make ourselves small in the face of the power held by other people or institutions. What can I do? How can I make a difference? The giant can grow in our perception until it is huge and covered in armor. But remember Goliath? He had a vulnerable spot. When we face giants, we need to focus on the places where we can make an impact and aim there, rather than try to face the giant head on. The story of David and Goliath underlines the need for giants and shepherds to end their power struggles and seek to be peers.

GIANTS WITHIN AND WITHOUT
❖ Lead a discussion with your class about the "giants" that people have to struggle with in your community (city, region). For example, what are some of the big issues, large forces, or overwhelming concerns that face you or others in your community? List these concerns on one half of a chalkboard or poster paper. On the other half, list some of the ways your church or individuals in your group might act as the "Davids" who stand in the face of the giant. Remember that David stood not for himself but on behalf of God to show everyone that the Lord was present!

Contemporary "Davids and Goliaths": What might be some contemporary scenarios of David and Goliath? Some examples might be: **(1)** nations with technological wealth and knowledge vs. nations with little wealth and failing

The Church—Giant or Shepherd?

As uncomfortable as it is to realize, many well-intentioned efforts for mission in the past have resulted in imposing North American and European cultural biases and Western assumptions on people around the world. Mission efforts into the new century hopefully proclaim the good news of Jesus Christ through the traditions and culture in which the church serves. The church has been seen as "the giant" in many communities because of its association with wealth, power, and political influence.

In its association with Western culture, the church has been seen as part of American or European national identity and thus is a giant by association. As U.S. citizens, we live in a nation that could be called the world's superpower. No matter how powerful or weak we ourselves feel, for much of the world, we are seen as the giant! As a church based in the United States, we would do well to remember this when we explore mission.

Hospitality Welcomes Everyone

While serving for the Board of Global Ministries with The United Methodist Church in Sierra Leone, West Africa, my husband and I often encountered situations that challenged our Western perceptions of the gospel. We learned a

economies, whose focus is survival rather than technological advancements; **(2)** a huge urban school district vs. a Spanish-speaking child and his or her parents; or **(3)** a multinational clothing company with overseas factories vs. an unemployed American worker on welfare. Discuss one of these examples or identify another. In such instances, what is the role of hospitality as justice?

THE CHURCH
❖ What are some ways that you might be seen by others as a "giant"? In your community, is the church considered a "giant" in any particular way? Discuss the pros and cons of being the giant.

Travel: Have you ever traveled outside North America and its territories? If so, how did the host nation perceive you as a US citizen? Did you find the same amenities or practices to which you are accustomed? How did you feel and respond?

HOSPITALITY WELCOMES EVERYONE

❖ Have you ever had or witnessed an experience similar to the ordination service misunderstanding? How can you prepare to avoid such mistakes in someone else's home?

❖ Reflect on the paragraph that begins, "Mission is about speaking and acting in ways that reflect the truth. . . ." Do you agree or disagree? Is mission about helping fearful people? What are the implications of this paragraph in a place, for example, like Sierra Leone, where the missioner disregarded the culture of the people? when the missioner is regarded as the "giant"? when the giant is also seen as an enemy?

❖ David faced the giant just with his sling and stone, "with who he was and what he had." What does it mean to face the giant concerns of our time in this way?

Invite a Guest: Consider inviting an active or retired missionary to talk to your

great deal about what it means to be a guest and to be hospitable as well. One experience was especially informative. It occurred during an ordination service for some of the students from the Theological Hall and Church Training Centre where we were on the faculty. The preacher was a missionary who had prepared his sermon in English. One of the students was translating for the congregation, many of whom were more comfortable in Krio, the language of daily conversations. The preacher urged the ordinands to be in ministry as shepherd of the sheep. He then instructed them to be good stewards of resources in their churches. The images were translated in this way: "Be like the man with the stick, who watches over the sheep and beats them when they do wrong. Also be like the man who works in the white man's house, cleaning and cooking."

Shepherds and stewards, in the context of the ordinary people of Sierra Leone, beat the sheep and cleaned rich people's homes! Clearly, important concepts were lost, and the whole task of ministry was bent beyond recognition— all for the missionary's failure to speak the gospel in the terms of the culture of which he was a guest.

Mission is about speaking and acting in ways that reflect the truth about the kingdom of God in a manner that is understood by those who receive the missioners. This kind of mission is nurtured through communication and relationship. Mission, in part, is about helping fearful people stand strongly, face to face with the giants who

64

church. Your denominational offices should have information on itinerating missionaries. Ask your guest to talk about the changing face of mission in this century. Look into becoming a supporting church for a missionary by contacting your denomination's mission office.

threaten their existence. Being a person in mission is being like David, who proclaims in the giant's face that he does not depend upon might, strength, swords, and threats, but upon the love and power of God!

When preparing to face Goliath, David was weighted down when he tried to dress like the soldiers in the army. When he simply faced Goliath with who he was and what he had, it was sufficient in the presence of God.

Back to Ourselves

Finally, let's reflect upon the story of David and Goliath more personally. What does the story teach us about our own efforts to make a difference, facing a hurting world? How can we stand before insurmountable problems and, through the power of God, not be overcome or flee in fear? How can we instead stand eye to eye, giant and shepherd together? There are four implications to this story that we can apply to our own spiritual practices as Christians.

■ We have what we need to be God's messengers and God's representatives. Fancy training, advanced study, extraordinary skills, official titles, and responsibilities have their place, but they are not necessarily most important when you face "the giant" or something that opposes and threatens to destroy. Courage and faith have an important role to play as well.

65

enemy, or foreigner? What barriers do these perceptions create, and what can be done about them?

Develop Faith Statements: Work together in pairs to develop a statement of faith based on the four implications of the David and Goliath story. You will want to articulate the statement personally and specifically. For example:

"I have what I need to be God's messenger because I can

_____.
I draw upon the spiritual power that is mine in Christ Jesus by _____.
I have been equipped with _____ to stand up to that which I fear.
Through God's power I will stand in a new relationship with _____, no longer afraid of _____."

HONORING THE STRANGER
❖ Read 1 Samuel 25:2-42. One of the features of biblical era hospitality that may seem strange to us is that a guest could invite him or herself or

■ When we draw upon the spiritual power given to us in God through Jesus Christ, we are already equipped to stand against evil. When we seek God's kingdom of equality, justice, wholeness, and peace, then we become God's agents and messengers, and God's power will prevail.

■ God has great things in store for those who are willing to stand up to the very things we fear. David cut off the giant's head, not out of vengeance, but to have it in hand to prove to the people that it was possible to overcome even the worst of one's fears and the most powerful destruction.

■ In contemporary terms, we may not slay the thing we fear or the enemy we face, but instead redefine our relationships, refusing to stand enemy to enemy. Instead we commit ourselves to live out the Jesus ethic, which tells us to "love our enemies." We look those we have called "other" eye to eye, and a new relationship is created.

Honoring the Stranger

David has more to teach us. On another occasion, David was in the wilderness with his troops and sought the help of a wealthy sheep owner, Nabal, to feed and shelter the men (1 Samuel 25:2-42). He sent some of the men to ask Nabal for supplies and food. Apparently, Nabal had no interest in

66

expect to be received with little or no notice. Which elements in the story present an understanding of hospitality different from your cultural expectations?

Study Biblical Hospitality: Review the information in "Biblical Hospitality" beginning on page 7. In what specific ways did Nabal breach the customs of hospitality? What could David have expected from Nabal? From what you know about the status of women, what risks was Abigail taking to accommodate David and his men?

❖ Abigail interceded before David could start his attack. This would have been an extreme and vindictive response, even though he had a right to expect some gesture of generosity from Nabal, who was clearly a wealthy man. What are the implications for being a good host and a good guest? (Neither man handled himself particularly well.)

being of help, especially to a bunch of strangers: "Shall I take my bread and my water and the meat that I have butchered for my shearers, and give it to men who come from I do not know where?" (1 Samuel 25:11).

This response infuriated David, for it was a profound breach of desert hospitality, and 400 of his troops prepared to attack. At this point Abigail, Nabal's wife, intervened and came bearing food and drink to David and his troops, apologizing profoundly and giving honor to David.

Abigail became in this story a symbol of hospitality. She risked her own personal safety to see that the needs of the stranger were cared for well. The name *Nabal* means "fool" and also refers to one who violates the social norms of etiquette and law. He clearly lived up to his name!

We live in a day and age when the stranger has become someone to treat with disdain or disregard. There are increasing incidents of road rage—anger expressed in explosive ways on the highways, almost always with strangers. Strangers are the persons children are told not to talk to or trust, to the extent that some children are frightened of any passerby. Strangers are anonymous and invisible, and often thought to be without worth, in much of contemporary North American culture.

To be hospitable is to honor the stranger, trusting in his or her inherent worth as a human being without needing to know any more about personal infor-

❖ Is hospitality simply a matter of etiquette? What is the difference between being nice to someone because you have to and extending care and hospitality to strangers simply because they are in your midst? Is the stranger someone you need? someone who will hurt you? someone who deserves honor? Explain.

mation. To serve God is to recognize the worth of persons who might be seen as enemies. It even means seeing them as God's anointed people. To honor the one who seeks to hurt you is the essence of hospitality. It means seeing the giant in human terms.

Parker Palmer speaks of the importance of strangers in his book *The Company of Strangers* (Crossroad, 1985). He says, "We gain a deeper understanding of our relation to the stranger when we remember that Jesus . . . identified himself with the sick, the prisoner, the stranger: 'Truly . . . as you did it to one of the least of these my brethren, you did it unto me.' . . . We can see how central is the stranger to the Christian conception of life. The stranger is not simply one who needs us. We need the stranger . . . if we are to know Christ and serve God, in truth and in love."

TRADITIONS OF HOSPITALITY
❖ What traditions of hospitality are central in your culture? (See also the story of the Tongan church in the next section.)

Tell Stories: What stories do you know of extraordinary generosity? What do those stories teach you about being gracious in the name of Jesus Christ?

Traditions of Hospitality

Hospitality is a way of being and seeing the world and does not always happen on one's own home turf. Consider one of the favorite hospitality stories of the Tongan people. The Kingdom of Tonga is a tiny cluster of islands near Fiji and Australia. It is the only remaining sovereign country in the Pacific. Their beloved Queen Salote attended the coronation of Queen Elizabeth and was the only reigning monarch present. On the day of the coronation, the rain poured down, yet she rode in an open carriage waving to the crowds. Queen Salote stole the hearts of the British people for her warmth and her generosity of spirit. And why did she ride in the rain when everyone else in the procession had a covered carriage? It was because the Queen of England rode in a covered carriage, and in the Tongan way, it would have been insulting to the Queen of England to ride in the same way. As an act of humility and respect, she kept her carriage open.

Hospitality is a mutual and interwoven relationship, which builds an ongoing respect among those who share it. This is the kind of hospitality that seems central to our life in the church.

Called and Commissioned

CALLED AND COMMISSIONED
❖ Prepare for this section by reading Acts 13–14. Saul (Paul) and the others who joined him encountered many situations in their mission work that influenced the kind of outreach they provided. (Acts 13:15 is an example of testing the stranger through speaking. Acts 13:42-52 indicates that they succeeded with some but not others.)

❖ Examine the three aspects of the call of these disciples. Discuss these sets of questions:

The establishment of the Christian faith in Tonga is wrapped up in the early 19th century missionary movement. Tongan church history describes the utter failure of the first missionary who came to Tonga. He arrived with an evangelistic plan to establish Christianity. He paid no attention to the culture and social structure of the Tongan people and tried to impose his own way. He lost his life in the effort!

The second missionary who came to Tonga spent time with the people. He realized how important the system of authority was in Tonga as well as the centrality of the king. The missionary focused, then, on the king. He spent time with the king and used language about Christianity that reflected the importance

(1) What is the role of the Holy Spirit in calling us to ministry? Have you been guided by the Spirit to do or be something? **(2)** What is the role of discernment and support of the sending congregation? **(3)** How does the community test, refine, and support a call to mission?

❖ The early church commissioned Saul and Barnabas to be sent out as preacher evangelists. What are some of the ways the church commissions its members for service today? What could be some new ways we could provide support for members in their service and ministry as Christians in their daily lives?

Invite a Guest: Invite a newly ordained clergyperson to discuss his or her ordination process. This process is intended to provide a community of guidance and commissioning for those going into ordained ministry.

Keep an Eye to Hospitality: Plan as a group to attend church next Sunday with "an

of kingship. Soon, the king was converted to the Christian faith, and then the royal household also. Then all of the people honored their king and converted. This second missionary was a British Methodist, and the Tongan Methodist church was born.

Appropriate mission and ministry begins within the context of the people who are to be served. It respects the community, honors the neighbor, and finds in the stranger the image of Christ. Mission that brings the good news of Jesus Christ is hospitable mission.

As the early church began its missionary work, the leaders were sent out by the church through "commissioning." In Acts 13:1-3, we read that, in the act of worship and fasting, the Holy Spirit spoke to the community, identifying Saul and Barnabas to be sent off for ministry away from home. Three aspects of this call are important.

First, the call for ministry happens in the context of worship. All genuine mission and ministry come from the intent of God and through the power of the Holy Spirit. There is a difference between responding to our own wants and needs and responding to the commissioning of the Holy Spirit. How does one understand the difference?

Second, the call comes within a discerning and ministering community. The community in the contemporary world incorporates not only the community from which one goes but also the community to which one is sent.

Third, ministry and mission are discerned within the community, tested and

70

eye to hospitality." In what ways is your church a place of hospitality, and in what ways does your church appear to lack hospitality? How can each member claim a ministry of hospitality?

Plan Worship: Together plan a worship service for the whole congregation that would provide recognition of the work people are doing, either in their jobs, their volunteer work, or in another aspect of their lives. Develop a way to affirm and commission people for their individual ministries. Perhaps this could be planned for the Labor Day weekend.

CLOSING

❖ Close with prayer: Almighty God of David and of Goliath, at times we shudder and shake as small, helpless creatures in the face of that which appears overwhelming and beyond our comprehension. At other times we puff ourselves up to impose our influence and authority in order to show we are right. Remind us we are empowered and sent by your strength and

refined in the context of community, and commissioned in the community of faith. The community knows an individual's skills and gifts and can help to mold the form of the ministry. This is an ongoing process.

There were times when Saul and Barnabas were threatened and attacked for the work they did. At one event in Lystra, Saul (Paul) was stoned and left for dead. The disciples "surrounded him" and he was then able to get up, go to the city, and then on to his next mission (Acts 14:20). This story may point to the reaffirmation of his ministry, and the testing of its direction within the community, in response to the attack.

When the work of Saul and Barnabas was rejected, they "shook the dust off their feet" and went on to the next place that needed them (Acts 13:51). When we seek out a situation in which we would like to be in mission and ministry, our first instinct should be towards hospitality. And as we have seen, hospitality is as much the responsibility of the guest as it is that of the host. If our outreach is not welcome, then we do not belong.

Parker Palmer is helpful once again. "This is what Jesus called for—hospitality to the sick and the hungry and the imprisoned without demanding that they become our friends or grateful allies, but hospitality in simple recognition of our unity with them, a unity which is both human and divine. Every hospitable act is an outward and visible sign of our inward and invisible unity, a unity which finds expression in the very root of the your might, which transform us into creatures of glory in your image. May we defend you all our days. Amen.

BIBLIOGRAPHY
❖ Robert McAfee Brown, *Unexpected News: Reading the Bible with Third World Eyes*, Westminster Press: Philadelphia, 1984.

❖ Megan McKenna, *Not Counting Women and Children: Neglected Stories from the Bible*, Orbis Books: Maryknoll, New York, 1994.

❖ Ernesto Cardenal. *The Gospel in Solentiname*, Orbis Books: a presentation of Bible stories from the perspective of persons in Latin America.

word 'hospitality,' for *hospes* means both host and guest—the two are really one."

We are called into a "hospes" community, where all are hosts and all are guests, where giants and shepherds meet without taking off each other's heads, and strangers and enemies save one another's lives. We are called to stand under a common consecration by the Spirit of the living God into a new unity with one another.

Session Five

$\mathcal{H}ospitality\ as\ a\ \mathcal{G}ift$

PURPOSE
The purpose of this session is to examine various stories of hospitality and to understand it as a gift both to the receiver and to the giver.

THE SESSION PLAN
Choose from among the core teaching activities and the extended session options to plan your session. **BOLD CAPS** indicate the text to which the activity relates. The icon ❖ identifies the core teaching options of the session. Add options in **Bold Italics** to extend your session beyond 45-60 minutes.

MEALS IN THE GOSPELS
❖ What does mealtime represent to you? Many families are fragmented by various activities and do not

$\mathcal{T}$here is a funny story about a teacher who asked the children in her class to bring something to school telling about their religious tradition. The Muslim child brought a prayer mat to show, the Catholic child brought a crucifix, the Jewish child brought a menorah, and the Protestant child brought a potluck dish! Indeed, sharing meals is an important part of church life for many people, and actually it was a significant part of Jesus' ministry.

Meals in the Gospels

There are numerous Gospel stories about Jesus sharing a meal with people. Jesus ate with his disciples; he gathered persons on the hillside for a meal; he ate with the disdained and immoral of the day—the tax collectors, the Roman leaders, and independent women. Jesus celebrated the Passover meal as an opportunity to open up new and deeper understandings of who he is. The post-

73

eat meals together. Does this cause something to be lost or missing in the family cohesion? In a family of one, meals are often solitary. If Christ is always present in the breaking of bread, is there such a thing as a table of one?

A MIRACLE MEAL
❖ Read John 6:1-14. What happens? What is the attitude of the disciples when it is clear they need to try to feed the crowd? How does this contrast with Jesus' attitude? Does the fact that there were doubtlessly even more people present than 5,000 (the women and children) make this story even more remarkable or incredible? Explain.

❖ What interpretations have you heard that "explain away" the story (for example, everyone had some food and the little boy inspired them to share)? Do you agree with any of these explanations? If this were easily explained, would it diminish what happened? Would it diminish the under-

Resurrection appearances in Luke and John include Jesus gathering persons around the breaking of bread, and in this action the risen Christ became known.

Mealtime is such a basic part of human existence and, in that sense, is a very personal experience. In Palestinian tradition, to eat a meal with someone was to make a covenant with that person for the year ahead. Jesus repeatedly made covenants of relationship with the most unlikely of people!

A Miracle Meal

While ordinary meals are central to the ministry of Jesus, the miraculous feedings are especially so. All four Gospels report on the miraculous meal for 5,000 persons. Matthew and Mark both include stories of feeding 4,000, evidently on another occasion. The account in John 6:1-14 is more clearly made to relate to the Eucharist, rising from the church setting familiar to John.

This Gospel report shows Jesus anticipating the people's hunger and both Philip and Andrew getting caught up in the logistics of finding food. They do not see that Jesus can provide more than ordinary food and is the best one to meet their needs. Matthew mentions 5,000 men present in the gathering, seated on the hillside. We know from modern scholarship that these 5,000 were also accompanied by at least twice as many women and children.

Jesus then took the simple food offered in hospitality by the young boy,

standing of God's
power in this incident?
Explain.

***Study Other Miracle
Meals:*** Look at the
other miraculous feed-
ing stories in Matthew
14:13-21; 15:32-39;
Mark 6:30-44; 8:1-10;
and Luke 9:10-17. How
do they compare? With
so many stories of the
same miracle, what
does this suggest to
you about its spiritual
importance?

blessed it in the manner of a host at a Jewish meal, and gave it to the guests. The five loaves and fishes become suffi-cient to feed the 15,000 or more people present. At the end there were 12 bas-kets left, perhaps representing the 12 tribes of Israel, but certainly demonstrat-ing the abundance possible through the blessing of Jesus and the boy's simple sharing of what he had.

A Christian Meal of Many Names

There are many names for the meal of the bread and cup, each of which has a theological meaning: Eucharist, meaning thanksgiving; Holy Communion, emphasizing the community gathered in union with Christ and one another; the Lord's Supper, commemorating the last supper of Jesus.

"Messianic Banquet" describes the theological idea that at the end of time, all will feast with the Messiah in a heavenly gathering of abundance. It is part of both Jewish and Christian tradition.

Hospitality as a Spiritual Practice

**HOSPITALITY AS
SPIRITUAL
PRACTICE**
❖ Discuss this definition
of hospitality in the first
paragraph. How are
hospitality and the king-
dom of God related?
❖ What does the story
of the difficult guest,

Hospitality based on the vision of the kingdom of God is a spiritual or holy practice. It isn't easy or clear or well defined. It has to do with relationships and mutual interdependence.

One community of people who understand the spiritual nature of hospi-

75

who prayed for and valued this community, teach you about hospitality? about the (perhaps unseen) fruit of your own acts of generosity? about extending yourself on behalf of others when they seem ungrateful or unaware? about complaining because of others? about the blessings of giving and receiving?

❖ What is your experience of having someone pray for you?

Pray This Week: Ask the class to write their names on a small piece of paper. At the end of the session, draw a name and ask them to commit that person to their prayers for the entire week.

❖ How does your vision of true community compare with Day's? Dorothy Day's challenge to "try to get to know each other, to learn of each other, to be part of a community over a meal, to serve and be served" provides a guideline for life in Christian community. What does it mean to you "to serve and be served"?

tality is the Catholic Workers, a national movement. The Catholic Worker Movement was founded by Dorothy Day in 1933 in the midst of the Depression, when she began to serve the poor of Manhattan's Lower East Side in New York by bringing people into her home. The people served by the Catholic Workers were always referred to as "guests." In the food kitchens and shelters, the guests were provided with the same hospitality that one would find in a private home.

In his book *The Call of Service* (Houghton Mifflin, 1994), which explores idealism and the urge to make a difference in the world, Robert Coles shares a number of stories about the Catholic Workers. He tells the story of one long-time guest, an alcoholic man who was often angry and difficult when he was at the table. One day he became quite ill and feared he would die. While waiting with a Catholic Worker at the hospital, the man shared how much the Catholic Workers meant to him.

The worker described the experience: "He told me how much he loved us, each and every one of us, and he said we are his only family, and we're all he's got, all he's had for years. And he told me that every day he goes into a church and says a long prayer for us. He sits in a pew and thanks God for us, for all who work in our hospitality house. . . . I was amazed, listening to him. I'd never before thought that carefully about what our guests think about us! I just assumed that they were grateful; and of

76

Invite a Guest: Invite someone with the Catholic Workers or some other shelter / hunger program to your church for conversation. See what needs they may have for ongoing support in which some in your group might participate.

course, Dorothy always talks about the gratitude *we* feel for the opportunity to be of service to others. . . . Suddenly, one of the men I'd always considered about as agitated and disturbed as anyone who came to us, . . . suddenly, that fellow turns out to be a daily supplicant at church for all of us."

Dorothy Day describes her vision of what it means to be truly a community: "I think we at the Worker believe it would be better for all of us . . . if we got to know each other, took an interest in one another. That is our ideal—what we try to do when we serve our meals. . . . So right here it's a challenge for us to try to get to know each other, to learn of each other, to be part of a community over a meal, to serve and be served. We serve, and they serve us by coming here—giving us the chance to serve, and so offering a service to us. . . . I think Isaiah and Jesus explained all this to us some time ago."

To learn of each other, to be part of a community over a meal, to serve and be served. These images of the spiritual practice of hospitality can guide and direct us as we claim our own hospitable ministry.

Christian Table Fellowship

TABLE FELLOWSHIP
❖ Read Paul's comments to the Corinthian church about the Lord's table in 1 Corinthians 11:17-34. What is the apparent intention of the meal?

The early church continued the tradition of feasting and meals as a Christian community, until apparently the practice got out of hand, and Paul, in his epistle to the Corinthians, intervened (1 Corinthians 11:17-34). There seemed to be persons in

77

What are the apparent abuses? What are some of the ways the body of Christ is divided over the Lord's table today?

❖ What is the difference between seeking an individual experience of the sacrament and seeking a community experience?

Do a "Fish Bowl" Discussion: Ask for two volunteers to role-play neighbors having a discussion over coffee. One starts with, "The important thing to me is my personal and private relationship with God. I don't have to go to church to worship God." The other person's stance is, "Of course I can talk to God alone, but I do it much better within the context of my church family." Others in the group will be silent spectators until the "neighbors" finish. Then, invite the observers to comment on the conversation and what truth it holds for them.

Review Your Communion Liturgy: Read the Communion ritual in your hymnal or

the community who arrived for the meals and treated them like an ordinary banquet. Persons with other work to do would arrive later and find there was no more food. Paul described for the Corinthians the difference between a meal that satisfies one's physical hunger and the "remembrance" that takes place in breaking the bread and sharing the cup.

There appears to have been a schism or divisions in the community over theological issues around the bread and cup. For some persons, the meals were beginning to take on a magical quality. For others, what apparently was important was the individual spiritual experience of receiving the meal of remembrance, rather than the community experience of the meal celebrated together. Paul ended his discourse reminding the community of the Last Supper and the words of Jesus. These are the words used throughout Christendom today in the celebration of the Eucharist. The invitation to the meal Paul offered to the early church is given to each of us as well.

Hospitality in Community

Luke's story of the post-Resurrection encounter with Jesus on the road to Emmaus provides another helpful framework to understand faith and mission in the context of hospitality. The story tells of two disciples traveling the seven-mile road from Jerusalem to Emmaus. They encountered a stranger who apparently didn't know anything about the events of book of worship. How does the liturgy inform your ministry of hospitality and mission?

HOSPITALITY IN COMMUNITY

❖ Read the account of the Emmaus experience in Luke 24:13-35. What happened? What are the elements of hospitality shown in this story? What are the elements of grace demonstrated by Jesus and others?

❖ Have you ever had an "Emmaus experience" when you suddenly recognized the presence of Christ? What was it like?

❖ Thinking about this and the First Corinthians reading, what do the two Scriptures teach about Jesus, the disciples, and us? What is the importance of the community in these references? the importance of the "stranger"?

the previous days and didn't understand their grief. The disciples explained the life and ministry of Jesus and how all was lost because of his death. The stranger taught them about the Scriptures in a way that "interpreted to them . . . the things" concerning Jesus. As they reached their destination and the stranger prepared to move on, the two disciples invited him to stay as their guest for a meal. It was at the meal that Jesus became known to them in the breaking of bread.

The stories from Luke and First Corinthians give us insight into Jesus, the disciples, and ourselves.

■ We meet Jesus as the one known in the context of the community, in the shared learning of the Scriptures, and in the meal, in the breaking of bread.

■ We experience the disciples as those who question who they are in relationship to what is happening around them and in light of teachings from the Scriptures and from Jesus. Christ is revealed to them in the stranger invited into the community to a meal.

We learn for ourselves about our own ministry of hospitality and ministry, which

■ takes place in community;

■ is informed by the Scriptures and the teachings of Jesus;

79

■ is acted upon in the relationship with the stranger, with whom "bread is broken";

■ is accomplished by recognizing in the stranger the presence of the risen Christ.

Participation in community, relationship with the stranger, being informed by Scripture, and sharing bread are the foundations upon which a faithful Christian discipleship is born.

Hospitality in Action

In his book *Unexpected News: Reading the Bible with Third World Eyes* (Westminster Press, 1984), Robert McAfee Brown sees in the Emmaus Scripture a guideline for engaged Christian living, in which the disciples move from talking about the meaning of what they know to acting out what they have experienced. He says, "For instead of continuing to *talk* about redemption, they *act it out*; they engage in a redeeming deed, inviting a total stranger to share a meal. . . . The shift is from truth talked about to truth lived out, from reflection to action. . . . Only when they break bread together, when they move from words to deeds, does clarity come." In breaking bread, a new relationship is created.

McAfee Brown warns against the tendency to avoid involvement and action until all the "facts" are gathered and all

HOSPITALITY IN ACTION

❖ Respond to McAfee Brown's statement beginning, "For instead of continuing to *talk* about redemption, they *act it out* . . . ." How was the disciples' action redemptive? What new relationship was created?

❖ At what point do you move from reflection to action? What does it take to get you involved in some kind of missional activity? What motivates you? Have you ever hesitated so long that you no longer had to act? If so, what was the effect? How might you or that situation have been different with your active engagement?

Examine what it means to be a person of action. Think of a need you consider pressing and develop an action plan to address that need in some specific and concrete way. Include a time line of action and consider the desired results. Be sure also to consider the spiritual dimension and purpose of your endeavor.

the analysis is completed, because too often people " 'postpone' the jump from thought to action" and do so for so long that "*not* to act *is* to act. It is to act by default for whoever is in charge." It may be part of the built-in rationalism of Western culture that so many of us get used to thinking we need to gather together all the information before we can "do" or "act." For instance, first we figure out what we think is right and then decide the actions that should result, or we decide what we believe and then "do" because of these beliefs.

We learn that to be "people of action" is

■ a way of living rather than a way of thinking;

■ being committed and caring rather than removed and analytical;

■ being involved rather than on the sidelines;

■ experiencing Christ "in the midst" rather than "away from it all."

A Personal Reflection on Finding the Holy

PERSONAL REFLECTION
❖ Have you experienced "the holy" in some surprising places? Where? Do you agree it is possible that the homeless man intended his drink as a sacred, hospitable gesture? If the offering is "impure," can the gesture be genuinely sacred or hospltable? Explain.

On one occasion, I had an opportunity to deliver some blankets to Glide United Methodist Church, which serves the needs of many persons who are homeless and in crisis in the Tenderloin of San Francisco. As I carried several

81

huge armloads of blankets into the building, a man who was waiting in the food line along the sidewalk stopped me. He looked at me, arms full of blankets, and said, "Now aren't you beautiful, aren't you beautiful!" He reached into his bag and pulled out his precious bottle of drink, in which he had already overindulged. He held it out to me and invited, "Here, have yourself a drink."

I politely refused and thanked him for his kindness before I made my way inside. Perhaps this is a rather extreme example, but there, in the action of this inebriated stranger, I experienced the presence of the risen Christ. He gave a gift of affirmation and kindness in response to my actions. He offered what he had to share in response. Perhaps it wasn't the most healthy and practical of offerings, but I had no doubt that it was meant with the sacredness of other holy meals.

God's Hospitality

Another biblical story, this time from the Old Testament, helps us further understand God's intention in our relationships with one another. The story comes out of one of the most traumatic times for the people of Israel, when the Babylonians invaded their beloved land. The Temple was destroyed, and the majority of the educated people and craftsman were taken into Babylon as captives.

The Hebrew people remained captives for decades, and new generations

---

Who Is Shut Out? Gather some old magazines, including news and mission magazines. Cut out pictures of persons who have been shut out in society. Draw an outline of a church on a large sheet of butcher paper. Glue pictures around the outside of the drawing. On the inside of the church, list ideas on ways that the doors can be opened to those who are shut out.

Write Your Reflections: Either during the session or as an at-home spiritual exercise, do some writing about your experiencing the holy or the sacrament in surprising ways. Invite volunteers to share their reflections with the whole group, but do not insist.

GOD'S HOSPITALITY
❖ Read Jeremiah 29:4-7. What did it mean to the exiles to seek the welfare of the (strange and foreign) city of an enemy and pray for its welfare? What does this passage teach you about God's hospitality?

about dealing with strangers and enemies? about the importance of understanding "home" as where God is rather than a place comfortable or familiar to us?

❖ How diverse is your community? your church? What are the benefits of entering someone else's "cultural living room" and experiencing life in a different way? What barriers or fears may prevent you from having the experience? What can you do to address those concerns?

❖ What are some ways that you can see your church, your community, and yourself "seek the welfare of others" who have been shut out?

thought only of the land of Babylon as home. The people implored God, "When will you save us and return us home?" They carefully preserved their traditions and community, removed from the Babylonian culture. They knew that one day the Lord would lead them back home to their promised land.

Finally, the word of God came to them through the prophet Jeremiah. It was the most shocking message they could possibly receive. "Thus says the LORD . . . to all the exiles . . . : Build houses and live in them; plant gardens and eat what they produce. Take wives . . . and give your daughters in marriage . . . ; multiply there, and do not decrease. But seek the welfare of the city where I have sent you . . . and pray to the Lord on its behalf, for in its welfare will you find your welfare" (Jeremiah 29:4-7).

God was giving them a home—right where they were. They were being told to open up their homes to the community in which they lived and to make it permanent. They were no longer a people on the move, but a people who were strangers in a strange land, which they would now call home. God's word of hope came, throwing open the flaps of their tents and the doors and windows of their lives to find mutual welfare with their world.

We live today in a world that can learn a lesson from the ancient Israelites. Many of us live in communities isolated from the dynamic reality of the world around us. Yet a brief venture out of our own community may provide an experience of driving across many nations of the world. In the part of the city where our family lives, we can find grocery stores and places of worship that reflect Chinese, Korean, Japanese, Middle Eastern, Russian, Euro-American, and African American traditions. The richness of the world has arrived at our doorstep, and God invites us to seek the welfare of others and take a look outside. Many persons in North America have been in danger of pitching our tents in a spiritual desert, becoming isolated and fearful of strangers in our midst. The church can provide an oasis in the desert and a shelter in the storm. It can be a place where the world can meet and learn to respect one another. God has called us to make our homes in unfamiliar places, across every boundary, in order to become God's own community.

Traditions of Hospitality

Hospitality can sometimes best be understood when viewed from the perspective of cultures and communities different from our own. As a missionary in Sierra Leone, I learned much about the ministry of hospitality. When my husband and I served there a decade and a half ago, it was counted among the world's poorest nations. Since that time there has been a substantial drop in economic welfare, and a civil war has devastated the nation. Yet the prevailing attitude is one of hospitality and faith in the provisions of God.

TRADITIONS

❖ Thinking again about the Gospel reports of the miraculous feeding, what traditions or customs do you know that express abundant hospitality? (Stories such as these seem plentiful from the era of the Great Depression.) Do you have any equivalent to keeping the extra bowl of food for the chance visitor? Is there something about being in mutual want that fuels a generous spirit? If you are not in want, what does this discussion suggest to you about being a guest or a host?

84

Times of cooking in Sierra Leone are communal, a time for women to learn together, and no one goes for water alone. Our screened home was an invitation for children to look through the windows to see what we were doing and for neighbors to walk by and call out friendly hellos.

Mealtimes were community times, and a Sierra Leonean meal of rice and sauce always served those present, with a bowl kept for the visitor who might stop by. When one was asked for a glass of water, it was a request for hospitality and was never to be refused. In Sierra Leone, water and rice became sacramental. Even in these troubled times, homes are opened for those who flee the war, and when one inquires what help is needed, prayers are usually requested.

WALKING HOME
❖ Examine the three conclusions about hospitality and mission and evaluate your experience with the entire study. What are your own conclusions about being in mission? about receiving and offering hospitality?

Walking Half-way Home

When one visits the home of someone in Sierra Leone and it is time to leave, the host does not say farewell at the door but instead leaves with the guests and walks with them half-way home. It seems a fitting image for the conclusion of our study on hospitality and mission:

■ Walking with one another between our places of living and working;

■ Sharing the journey of another's life and struggle;

■ Accompanying one another for protection and guidance.

CLOSING
Serve Communion:
Arrange for Holy
Communion or a love
feast as the closing of
your time together.

❖ Close with prayer:
"Jesus, be known to us
in this gathering and in
the breaking of bread
with family and friends
in our daily meal. May
we seek to find you, be
for you, love for you,
and finally come to
know you throughout
all our days. Amen."

As Christians, we know we experience a spirit of generosity in our lives. Our goal is to educate and enhance that spirit in spite of our fears about where this may lead us. As we work to express our compassion and love, we want to make sure it is received, seen, and heard—and we want to avoid misunderstanding. As we walk alongside people who are different or in need, we listen and we learn. We grow in our ability to offer them the blessings and hospitality of Jesus Christ, remembering that hospitality takes place within the community of God.